Live Out Love takes you to the depths and helps you rise above the hard in this world—all while inspiring us to live a little louder for God. Angelise's message points straight to the Father heart of God. She knows revival starts in our own heart and conveys this truth brilliantly. This book will give you a fresh spark you didn't know you needed, leaving you radiant and ready to reveal Christ to others as your life is lived out loud for Him.

— Amy Elaine Martinez, Host of The Grace Frontier Podcast, Author of *Becoming a Victory Girl* and Founder of Amy Elaine Ministries.

I've known Angelise and her family for a long time and this book is like she is: inspiring, convicting, and full of the Word applied to the heart. If you are a person who wants to make a difference or who has a desire for things to be different, this book is for you. My prayer is that, like me, you will be convicted and inspired by the Spirit and the Word as you read this book, and find the grace for change that only comes from words delivered by someone who has lived them.

— Bruce Ho, Senior Pastor of Every Nation Taipei

Angelise's vulnerability and teachable spirit will challenge you to dig deep within your own heart. If you will let them, Angelise's words will help to transform you into the unique fingerprint of God's love you were created to be.

— Brooke Hamlin, Author of *The Good Portion* and *Escaping Ordinary*

Live Out Love is a great reminder of how simple the gospel truly is. Angelise gives great tools in this book to apply to our everyday lives to help us truly live out the gospel. I believe this book will bring much needed conviction to the hearts of many Christians and the Body of Christ as a whole. I have watched Angelise first hand live out what she is preaching in this book. She is quick to humble herself, recognize her faults and allows Jesus to correct her. This book speaks from the deepest places of her heart because she has walked through the fires of this life and continues to do so daily! *Live Out Love* is for every Christian, and also for any Christian who has walked away from the Church. It is a heart cry to reach not only the lost but to help bring back the prodigals who have become too battle weary by the very people they should be able to trust, Christians.

— Kristin Lynnea Taylor, Founder of Living the Kingdom Way

I believe the author has captured the parts of the Word of God that best deals with relationships and how to live out love in our lives and win souls. Each chapter, from the first to the eleventh, has great words on how we are to live out love-first to ourselves and then to others, family, and friends. I particularly like the part where it talked about active listening as one of the most powerful expressions of love. Constantly glued on our smartphones, we have allowed digital distractions to displace us from the here and now of life, making active listening a lost art. This book encourages us to repent and ask God to heal our eyes to be patient, kind and longsuffering and to actively listen.

— Rev. Dr. Charles Rasberry, LCC Clinical Supervisor
and Founder of Oasis for Life Wellness Center

In *Live Out Love,* Angelise writes beautifully about our Christian call to humility, action and truth. This book is an important one for anyone serious about living out their Christian witness well. With empathy, grace and vulnerability, Angelise offers sound wisdom and Biblical guidance for the modern Christian–and it couldn't be more timely.

— Ericka Andersen, Author of *Reason to Return: Why Women
Need the Church & the Church Needs Women*

OUR WITNESS SPEAKS LOUDER
THAN OUR WORDS

ANGELISE SCHRADER

Live Out Love —Copyright ©2023 by Angelise Schrader

Published by UNITED HOUSE Publishing

All rights reserved. No portion of this book may be reproduced or shared in any form–electronic, printed, photocopied, recording, or by any information storage and retrieval system, without prior written permission from the publisher. The use of short quotations is permitted.

Scripture quotations marked (NIV) are taken from the Holy Bible, New International Version®, NIV®. Copyright © 1973, 1978, 1984, 2011 by Biblica, Inc.TM Used by permission of Zondervan. All rights reserved worldwide. www.zondervan.com The "NIV" and "New International Version" are trademarks registered in the United States Patent and Trademark Office by Biblica, Inc.TM

Scripture quotations marked (NLT) are taken from the Holy Bible, New Living Translation, copyright ©1996, 2004, 2015 by Tyndale House Foundation. Used by permission of Tyndale House Publishers, Carol Stream, Illinois 60188. All rights reserved.

Scripture quotations marked ESV are from the ESV® Bible (The Holy Bible, English Standard Version®), copyright © 2001 by Crossway, a publishing ministry of Good News Publishers. Used by permission. All rights reserved. The ESV text may not be quoted in any publication made available to the public by a Creative Commons license. The ESV may not be translated into any other language

Scripture quotations marked MSG are taken from The Message, copyright © 1993, 2002, 2018 by Eugene H. Peterson. Used by permission of NavPress. All rights reserved. Represented by Tyndale House Publishers.

Scripture quotations marked MSG are taken from The Message, copyright © 1993, 2002, 2018 by Eugene H. Peterson. Used by permission of NavPress. All rights reserved. Represented by Tyndale House Publishers.

ISBN: 978-1-952840-39-5

UNITED HOUSE Publishing

Waterford, Michigan

info@unitedhousepublishing.com

www.unitedhousepublishing.com

Cover photograph : Harriet Hui

Cover layout and interior design:

Anna Hilton, anna-hiltondesigns@gmail.com

Printed in the United States of America

2023—First Edition

SPECIAL SALES

Most UNITED HOUSE books are available at special quantity discounts when purchased in bulk by corporations, organizations, and special-interest groups. For

To my Papa
who always heard my heart

Table of CONTENTS

Foreword by Shay Arthur, *Iris Global* i

Introduction: The Fruit of Listening ix

Oversalted 1

The 3 Most Powerful Words 19

The Heart Behind it All 31

Just One Piece of the Puzzle 43

Work of the Spirit 57

Get Out of the Way 73

Good Does Not Equal God 87

Making New Wineskins 101

The Power of Repentance 119

Let My Life Be the Proof 139

Our Secret Weapon 149

Live Out Love

FOREWORD BY SHAY ARTHUR

As I read this book, a common thought kept crossing my heart and mind: "Where was a book like this in my early 20s?" It was like reading a handbook for everything I wish I had words for in those foundational years of life. I said a simple prayer to Jesus when I was young and asked Him to come and live in my heart and to have His way in my life. At such a young age, I definitely did not know what all that would entail. It was the best choice I made, and it was also the costliest choice. No one told me that following Jesus would come with hardship. No one sat me down and told me it would cost me everything. Instead, I often heard about God's blessings and His peace and joy. As one-sided as it seems, they are also correct. Later in life, when I started experiencing the cost of following Jesus, I found myself in a difficult position. There was this growing tension of figuring out how to follow

Jesus happening inside me. I know that in following Jesus, there are tremendous blessings and promises that will outlast my lifetime, as His words will go beyond me. I also learned in my Bible that God's promises would not easily be handed to me. It was not going to come from making faith statements. His promises would come from spending time in the presence, growing in Him, and wrestling out tensions with Jesus. It is true to say that God will never leave me, but I also know that I'm not meant to walk on roses all the time. When I started reading my Bible as someone who wanted to grow and look like him and not just reap His benefits, I started seeing that there was something I had been missing out on. I think many believers are scared to tell people that it will cost them everything to follow Jesus. It is easy to say "yes" to a God with promises and benefits, but it is not so easy to say "yes" when you realize that it will come with losing yourself along the way.

I have come to deeply appreciate it when someone shares the full Gospel with me that invites me to receive God's amazing grace and love and share in Christ's sufferings. In *Live Out Love*, Angelise gives us insight into the tension we will face as we follow Jesus and allow Him to be the catalyst for our healing. Jesus takes our breadcrumbs that we feel we give Him, and He feeds the community around us. He takes our hearts, softens them, and makes them look like Himself. He is not scared of our messes. He does not seek perfection from us. He will complete the good work He began in us long ago. Jesus isn't up there yelling at us. He is nudging us along by His *foreward*

Spirit and His power so that we can become His disciples who make disciples and spread the good news all over the earth. It blesses me on a deep level that Angelise is not scared to talk about the messy, hard truths and tensions of leveraging our lives and hearts for God. He will use our brokenness to heal others. There is a beauty in the mystery of what she captures through these pages that will accelerate you into leveraging your life for God and be a willing vessel for the healing of others around you. Following Jesus will cost you everything, but it is worthy of everything you could ever give. In our culture, we want quick fixes and instantaneous happenings. These things are not impossible, but when you realize that God is after your heart more than anyone else, you will realize that your breakthroughs and healing will always take more time than you desire. When you can make peace with this, you will be less likely to get angry at God. Instead, choose to surrender to the process of His trustworthy hands. There must be a place where we can talk about the full Gospel. We cannot shy away from sufferings and must be reminded that they have an expiration date because of Christ's glorious overcoming that took place on the Cross. We cannot just expect to live in the complete resurrection without self denial. This is the tension of our day.

As we live in the days of self help and self care, I am concerned that in our selfish ambitions, we will forget just how beautiful it is to yield to God and trust Him to take care of us. Don't hear me wrong; I must continually learn how to rest and get help from mentors and those ahead of me on this journey. There is a place of safety in Him and others that allows you to receive healing and take the time you need to recover. I am not saying to lose yourself to others around you. I am saying to lose yourself in Him; the Maker and Creator of your heart. The one who knows how you tick and how you need to rest better than you ever could. This is what it means to be a catalyst. This is what it means to be a disciple of Christ. The world needs to see

Christ's reflection in us. This takes time. This takes risk. This takes faith. This is not an easy thing to walk out. This is not for the faint of heart, but it is for anyone willing to go all in with Jesus. It is for those that have come to the end of themselves and have nowhere else to go. This is for those that want to see transformation happen in profound ways that will outlast themselves. The world screams that change comes from self discovery, but we know as Jesus followers that real deep transformation comes from looking at Jesus. Transformation does not come quickly; the deeper it goes, the greater the fruit it will bear. Many want a quick change, but Christ bids us come and let Him go deep so that the fruit will outlast our lives.

I am reminded of the scripture, "This same Good News that came to you is going out all over the world. It is bearing fruit everywhere by changing lives, just as it changed your lives from the day you first heard and understood the truth about God's wonderful grace" (Colossians 1:6). The Good News that has transformed your life is still going out all over the world.

foreward

It bears fruit everywhere by changing lives the same way it has changed yours. This is encouraging to me because the hard times of growing in Christ will pay off by spreading continually to those around me when I become a witness of this glorious Gospel. We are not to be shy when we share the Gospel. We are to be quick to speak of Jesus as much as possible. We will not back down from sharing about the testing and the tensions of following Him. We will also be quick to share the fruit it bears in our hearts and communities. This is what it means to be someone leveraging themselves to be a catalyst for Christ. This is what you were made for. You were made for Him and are capable of so much when He is at the center of your life. You can truly trust His ways and His heart towards you that causes you to lay down and get lost in His face. You can bring Him the brokenness of life and its challenges, knowing He is gentle and lowly. You can also know that He will cause everything to work out for your good. We typically want Him to do it the way we think is good, but it usually does not work that way. You were still made to surrender. You won't even graduate surrender. The times we think we arrive are the times we become religious. That is not your portion. You were made to accomplish hard things. You were made to see the Kingdom come to earth in ways only you can. You were made to be loved and love those around you. My friends, do not overcomplicate what He started in you. You cannot finish what you did not start in yourself. Let He who began a good work complete it within you and be quick to allow Him to use your life to touch others!!! You are meant to be a catalyst for Christ. Jesus showed us what it was to be a catalyst; we can do this because He has given us a model and example. As you read this book, I pray that you would yield to the One that is greater than you and let Him be the potter of your life. I pray that you would find the person of Jesus in these pages and sense His ever nearness and delight in you. I pray that you would lay it all down for the sake of Heaven coming to Earth and see your heart, your family, and your region transformed to be a catalyst for Christ.

Shay Arthur, Senior Leader, *Iris Global*

The fruit of LISTENING

I am the product of a father who listened. Even in the moments when I knew he wanted to pull his hair out, he instead allowed me to take my crazy questions one step deeper. The most profound spiritual lessons were learned in those hard moments. I was changed because someone took the time to hear my heart, acknowledge my struggle, and love me right in the midst of it. I have often said I am a Christian today because of the example of my father's love. He was the kind of father who listened before he spoke. He wanted to know my heart before He tried to fix my problems.

We are each called to live abundant lives of healing (John 10:10). Our lives should testify that Christ came for our freedom (Galatians 5:1). But when we walk around judging people, we turn them away from the kingdom rather than drawing them in. The way my dad loved me is the way we are each called to love someone else.

live out love

Did you know who you have been divinely designed to pour life and love into others? Each one of us was created to change the environments we walk into. We were given two ears so that we can better listen to hearts longing to be known. We each have been equipped with unique giftings, tools if you will, to expand the Kingdom of God on earth. You were made to demolish the kingdom of darkness and bring souls into His glorious light. Are you using your spiritual arsenal the way it was made to be used?

We can become instruments of destruction and confusion when we preach more than we love. When we try to fix people without first loving them in their brokenness, we can make the healing process take much longer than it should. As much as I've had loving examples like my father who created space for me to grow and change, I've also experienced people who knew the truth I needed but tried to make me hear it on their terms and on their timeline. Instead of preparing the difficult pill of conviction in a way that was easy to swallow, they gagged me on the truth, even as I fought to let it seep into my heart. They tried to force God's truth in places the Holy Spirit had not yet prepared. I so badly wanted to let His truth change my wayward heart. But without the love I needed, the pill did not go down easily. So the truth circled my mind until the right time, when someone lovingly reminded me Whose I was. There is something about love that paves the way for truth to be swallowed.

My heart is crying out for the Church today because we spend far too much time arguing with each other about things that don't really matter and judging those outside of our walls.

the fruit of listening

We have missed out on the big picture: helping the lost get found. This has been the painful wakeup call of my life, again and again. I believe the broken places of my life are becoming a platform for Him to display His strength. May my honesty about my mistakes prove to be the very ingredient that sets free other catalysts for healing. You were made to bring hope to your family, neighbors and community.

There is a dying world out there, and it's time for us to start discipling those He puts into our paths. It's time for the Church to learn the art of listening so she can rise up and become the force she was designed to be. We are called to be people who love when it's hard, listen well, and create space to help others experience the freedom for which Christ paid a heavy price.

We are not simply exiles here, but agents; emissaries sent on a specific special mission to live God-exalting lives that bring hope to those around us. We aren't lame sojourners, but equipped worshiping instruments pointing to a powerful, Almighty God.

The world is crying out for a hero; someone to come and break the spell sin has cast on us. The good news is, He came, and He paid the price on a rugged cross. We are no longer under the law of sin and death. Hallelujah! But too many of us have covered up the heart of His message, knowingly or unknowingly, with our agenda. We have let our unhealed and broken old identities do the talking. We have tried to fix others on our terms. We have taken our half-truths and wounded perspectives and lathered them with the Bible to try and make people good.

We have forgotten the power of transformation that comes from a life surrendered to the voice of the Holy Spirit. Because of this, we have injured more people than we have healed. Our legacy as "Church" in America speaks loudly of legalism rather than the power of transforming, Agape love. We were called to create space for people to experience the love of God that convicts their sin and changes their lives. It's our humility and obedience that allows Christ in us to do the healing and changing. This only happens when we lay down our rights, surrender our perspectives and walk in obedience. In our weakness, He is made strong.

Let's look at this principle when it comes to a medical diagnosis. There is a proper order and process required to address a health issue. First, we assess what is going on. Then, we come up with a plan and a team to resolve the problem. After the difficult and strenuous journey through surgery, you finally move towards post-care healing.

We mess up the order when we come in with our plans. Perhaps, hypothetically, you have tried to diagnose a patient who is already in surgery? At this point, God has begun the process of identifying their blind spots and bringing conviction, but you are speaking to them as if they are unaware of their mistakes and hence, re-injuring their already convicted heart. Or maybe you are that Christian attempting to speak recovery to someone who is still under spiritual anesthesia? You are comforting and downplaying areas of conviction where God actually wants to do deep uprooting, re-aligning and correcting. Stop!

the fruit of listening

We bring confusion to His order when we step out of alignment and speak without first assessing the situation through His lens. He is big enough for this case. He knows where someone is and what they need to step into wholeness. And when we step in, outside of submitting to His voice and lead, we delay the process. He knows when a listening ear or a word of correction is needed. It's His love that changes lives. It's our job to work with Him.

Those people who are hurting in your life don't just need to hear the truth. They need to see the example. They need to know you hear them. They need to know you love them. They need to see your obedience in the face of opposition and trial. The world will know we are Christians by what we do. When they see us love in the hard places, when human strength would give up, people will stop and take notice. That's when they know something supernatural is taking place. That's when they will want a taste of whatever it is you and I have.

It's because of the living, breathing witness in others that I have been changed. It is in our bearing witness to a Greater Love that those who watch us will be transformed. We aren't called to the kind of love that culture frivolously throws around but instead to sacrificial love- even when it hurts. That can only flow from us if we are securely rooted in His love for us and can trust Him to fight for us when our circumstances say otherwise.

So how can we learn to be vessels who create space for God to move and bring about healing in our families and communities? What does it mean to be the salt of the earth?

live out love

What does it mean to be a new wineskin? How do we train ourselves to become facilitators of God's healing oil here on Earth?

Join me as we dig in to learn together how to become catalysts for healing in our communities.

1

Oversalted

> Walk in wisdom toward outsiders, making the best use of the time. Let your speech always be gracious, seasoned with salt, so that you may know how you ought to answer each person.
> Colossians 4:5-6, ESV

I remember being a young bride and having some of our first guests over for dinner. I wanted everything to be perfect. The table was set, the shopping list was handled in advance, and the final presentation of the food was timed to correspond within fifteen minutes of our guests' arrival. The house smelled amazing, and I was ready to show off my new "wife skills."

Then came the first course: a homemade salad, complete with a dressing that I had made from scratch. My mom is a queen in the kitchen at creating elaborate flavors for the palate, especially in salads, so I learned from the best. Every good salad must have an oil base. Our preferred vinaigrette concoction usually includes olive oil and a red or balsamic vinegar. There's something delicious about mixing a neutral and fatty olive oil with an electric and tangy vinegar. The combo creates something uniquely appetizing. From there you can add any slew of spices.

My mother and I like to keep it simple: garlic powder, pepper and salt.

Salt is a good thing. It adds flavor and brings out the layers of a dish. It also has many health benefits. The right amount in the body helps you stay hydrated, promotes good vascular health, balances electrolytes, prevents muscle cramping, supports a healthy nervous system, and improves sleep.

However, too much salt destroys the same recipe. Ever heard of "over seasoning"? It's a classic first-time wife rite of passage. Lather enough of this savory spice, and you will have to throw everything away. None of the nutrition on the plate is absorbed. What was meant to enhance the flavor could actually destroy it, and those sitting at your table will be unable to swallow what is being served. Embodying the "brand new hostess initiation" at that dinner, my oversalting had destroyed all the satisfying parts of the salad.

Does this not also apply to the way we communicate our faith to our friends, neighbors, spouses, and kids? Do we know how to properly season the presentation of our beliefs when it comes to our Christian witness? The same ingredient meant to enrich, strengthen and add flavor, can also become a harsh addition when used without the wisdom, precision and patience of a master chef.

Salt that Burns

The same salt that can elevate an unexceptional recipe, can also be overused. What can bring health and flavor in small doses, can lead to crippling health issues when used in abundance. Long-term oversalting can lead to headaches, enlarged heart muscles, heart failure, high blood pressure, kidney disease, kidney stones, osteoporosis, stomach cancer, and strokes. This same principle applies to how we use the salt of correction in our relationships with others. Helpful input from well-meaning believers that was meant to bring truth that convicts and changes, can be misapplied and cause long-term soul pain and division.

Oversalting is the enemy's version of "religion;" one that appears godly, but does not bear the fruit of His spirit. It sounds right, it looks right, but the inside is just our flesh attempting to play God. Instead of bringing flavor to the gospel, it stings the raw places in people and causes further heartache. Instead of flavoring our interactions and causing seekers to want to learn more, it stings vulnerable heart wounds and pushes people away from the Lifegiver. It's that feeling that rubs you the wrong way when you are wrestling through deep discouragement, and a well- meaning Christian pats you on the shoulder and says, "The joy of the Lord is your strength."

I am a recovering oversalter. I'm a lover of scripture. I love His Word, and sometimes that obsession can come off as obnoxious instead of tasteful. There was a social media photo that was going around a couple years ago that I found myself re-posting once (and then quickly remembered this oversalting principle and took it down). It read: "It's not that Christians want to shove Jesus down your throat, but man if YOU KNEW. If you KNEW how He can transform you, how He can take away all that bitterness, that sorrow, that hurt, that depression, anxiety. We boast about our Lord because He is MIGHTY!"

My heart sees a post declaring the goodness and might of my God. The heart behind this post is wanting to brag about who God is and all He has done. But if we are honest with ourselves and ask for outside accountability and input from wise older believers, this post really feeds the flesh rather than our spirit. Why do I say this? Because we shouldn't have to brag. We shouldn't have to prove who God is or force someone else to get it. Who He is in us should be something that people can taste without us having to explain the flavor. It's why sales people get such a bad wrap when they overpush a product. The harder you push, the more it's apparent that perhaps you don't believe your own story. Others should be asking us more about Jesus because His presence is inviting them. His convicting and loving care in our lives should cause others to ask what is different. They were made by Him to be loved by Him. We don't have to shove it. He invites us in rather than pushing us to imbibe. When we post things like this, our salt has a burning effect.

Oversalting has displayed itself in my marriage when I have been impatient with God's timing to shift situations; when I've tried to use my words as an attempt to fix immediately what was off in the environment. My husband, Matt, has often told me, when I am in one of my pious moments, "You are making it worse." And that is exactly what my desire to talk about the gospel instead of live it out has done on more than one occasion: delayed healing and made everything messier.

oversalted

His Truth is crucial, but too many people have been turned off by the news of the gospel I carried in my soul because I talked more than I walked. I preached more than I loved. Why? Because it is so much easier. It's easier to post than to make time to listen to another perspective. It's more comfortable to hold on to the flesh and try to fix someone without the sacrifice of self. But that, my friends, is known as hypocrisy. Our world has seen enough double-sidedness and pride from Christians. They need to see believers who are living sacrifices (Romans 12:1). They need to see Christians who reflect their savior God who became man and put Himself on a cross for undeserving sinners.

This is such a difficult blind spot to reveal. It's tricky to put your finger on what is off. Many of us can go through life without our facade of self righteousness ever being called out. But God, in His mercy, gave me a husband who doesn't have an overly spiritual bent, so any time my faith plays out in a way that was me and not God, he is the first one to point it out. My Christian resume did not impress him in the slightest. He cared about, from me, relational authenticity and the ability to humble myself when I failed. What an annoyingly hand-picked gift of sanctification (aka the process of helping me look more like Christ).

My response was, of course, to embrace his "call outs" as a gift from God. NOT! At first I questioned if he in fact was a gift from the enemy. How dare he call out the blind spots in me!

But time has revealed just how good God has been to answer my heart's cry of "Jesus, make me look more like you!" And the best way to do that, is to reveal all the places in me not like Him.

The Church has been called out a lot these days for not living what we preach and talking about holiness more than living it. The reason why deconstructionism is gaining so much traction is not just because of the sin in men's hearts. We, the Body of Christ, have a part to play. We have been so busy doing ministry that we have forgotten that our witness to those closest to us is our most important ministry. The wounds of the last generation are the evidence of our failure. Too many have heard the gospel but have been burned by the inconsistency and lack of humility from those who claimed to walk with Him.

Do you feel any sting of conviction on this charge? Are you trying to downplay, even right now, its ability to hit home in your heart? Instead of getting defensive and giving justifications, what we are actually called to do is own up to our need for Jesus and extend the same grace He gives us for our violations against Him. Just as others' sins can't be justified, neither should ours be. We must all live open, vulnerable and honest about our brokenness. But for Jesus, there go I. Any other response is legalism – where we move from servant to judge.

Salt that Enhances

In Colossians 4, Paul is writing to a church in Colossae about walking in their new identity. He ends his instruction to them by reminding them to walk with wisdom when it comes to outsiders (those not a part of their Christian church community). And what is the roadmap for interacting with their prime mission field? "Always be gracious and seasoned with salt, so they may know how to answer each person" (Colossians 4:6, ESV, emphasis added).

The gospel is the same truth yesterday, today, and forever. Jesus came into our broken world to convict us of our sin and restore us to relationship with Him. It's a simple, yet hard truth. No one likes to be told they've got problems. No one wants to hear they are the issue. And the reality of the matter is, telling people they are in need of repair rarely accomplishes anything. Think about the areas in your life in which you have struggled most and needed healing or a breakthrough. Did transformation happen when somebody told you that you had an issue with watching too much TV, gossipping about neighbors, not doing what you preach, or spending too much money on things to fill the emptiness in your soul? Probably not.

Romans reminds us that " . . . God's kindness is meant to lead us to repentance" (Romans 2:4, ESV). Yes; this verse has often been labeled as one misapplied by church leaders. Some have argued that certain sects of the Christian faith use this as an excuse for avoiding addressing shortcomings at all. And while for some this may be true, perhaps we have been too hard-hearted to hear the conviction of these words for our own souls.

I fear much of the Church has categorized itself into two camps: those who love truth and those who love grace. Instead of seeing the other for the strengths brought to the whole body, we have pointed fingers and cut ourselves off from members who carry the balancing flavor we need. God is grace and truth all wrapped up into one. He speaks convicting truth with lovingkindness at the exact same time, and if we lean towards our preferred mode of operation, we miss out on becoming the Body of Christ He designed.

Every one of us judges, as Romans 2, spells out plainly: "Therefore you have no excuse, O man, every one of you who judges. For in passing judgment on another you condemn yourself, because you, the judge, practice the very same things. We know that the judgment of God rightly falls on those who practice such things" (Romans 2:1-2, ESV). These are the verses that lead into the reminder that it is His kindness that draws us to repentance.

Some of us have heard these words too many times and lost the meaning behind them. The phrasing is so different from our current vernacular. I found The Message Bible's translation of Romans 2, helpful in understanding the heart behind what Paul was writing. The fresh wording gave this passage new life in convicting me.

> Those people are on a dark spiral downward. But if you think that leaves you on the high ground where you can point your finger at others, think again. Every time you criticize someone, you condemn yourself. It takes one to know one. Judgmental criticism of others is a well-known way of escaping detection in your own crimes and misdemeanors. But God isn't so easily diverted. He sees right through all such smoke screens and holds you to what you've done. You didn't think, did you, that just by pointing your finger at others you would distract God from seeing all your misdoings and from coming down on you hard? Or did you think that because he's such a nice God, he'd let you off the hook? Better think this one through from the beginning. God is kind, but he's not soft. In kindness he takes us firmly by the hand and leads us into a radical life-change.
>
> Romans 2:1-4, The Message

oversalted

I love the phrasing of verse 4: "God is kind, but He's not soft." This reminds me of when I'm parenting my kids. If I allow them to continue to ignore me when I call and sass me with no consequences, they learn that Mom is kind, but also soft, so they can walk all over her. If all I do is require obedience, never engaging with their frustrations and their heart needs, then their experience tells them that Mom is not kind or soft. The gospel calls us to blend kindness and softness in a way that brings transformation. Boundaries and real-life consequences paired with a heart that cares create space for life-giving truth to be absorbed; not because of the fear of consequences, but because they know it is a way that brings them life.

This is the gospel. This is why Jesus had to come. This is why we don't get what we deserve. Still, we aren't given a license to do whatever we want either. He is the King of endless forgiveness, but He isn't a God to be taken advantage of or made a fool. There is a price to be paid for sin. And He paid it. Being able to partake in that glorious actuality will lead to a radical life change.

This is what it's all about. When Paul called us to "always be gracious," He was calling us to remember Romans 2. It is Christ's kindness that drew us to repentance. It's Christ's overwhelming love that helped us accept the hard fact that we desperately need Him. This is not a watered-down truth. It is the flavor of gentleness that draws others to Him.

Too often we use our truth-slinging as an excuse to forego basic human kindness and Holy Spirit-inspired mercy. When each of us remembers He chose us not because of what we have done but because of who He is, it reveals our double standard of judgment, and this illumination should transform the way we show graciousness to others. His truth has radically transformed our reality. Therefore, we should always be gracious to outsiders. For this is how He interacts with us. He calls us to not just represent His truth, but to represent His heart.

Salt that Transforms

When salt dissolves in water there is actually a chemical change. What was once sodium chloride and hydrogen oxide, becomes a salt water or brine. It takes a powerful force of reverse osmosis to bring the two back into their original states.

Isn't this what we are longing for in our Christian walk? The right salt and water combo that actually transforms us from humans toting a Bible to believers who speak His Truth with grace in season. My counselor calls it growing from a house of thoughts into the image of Christ. It's Christ's transformation in us that allows the salt to do its work. True healing requires hard honesty and gracious compassion in order for breakthrough to happen.

When the doctors found a malignant tumor on my two year old son in the fall of 2018, I wanted to know exactly what he had. I didn't want a watered down version of a diagnosis that tiptoed around the issue. I didn't want them to tell me he had a cold and send me home with some cough syrup. We would call that medical malpractice. I needed to know exactly what they had found, no matter how bad. At the same time, I did not appreciate

oversalted

doctors we met who lathered everything in worst case scenarios. I wanted them to communicate in a way that addressed the situation factually and then move on to the options at hand for a cure. I needed them to tell me the truth, and I needed them to do it with kind compassion. The best doctors carry good bedside manner paired with a robust understanding of the disease.

This is what Paul means when he tells us to season with salt. We have to share the truth, but in a way that is compassionate to those hearing the hard diagnosis: they are sinners desperately in need of a Savior. We aren't called to water down the truth till it is unrecognizable, and yet we have to communicate in a way that acknowledges just how hard the news of conviction is to swallow.

There have been so many people in my life who have spoken the truth, but it was spoken from a place of trying to fix me instead of trying to help me heal. Because it was wrapped in their timeframe, for their agenda, valuable nuggets fell on hurting ears, and a breach was caused as I struggled to take in what I knew was true. It's hard to swallow over-seasoned food; isn't it?

Salt is candor. It brings out the flavors of a meat. It highlights the layers of a dish. Food would be bland without it. The gospel truth I need to hear daily is not only that I am a sinner desperately in need of a Savior, but also the encouraging hope that God has done what we could not on our own. My misdeeds have been overcome at the cross because of His sacrifice. He has lifted the unbearable yoke of our depravity. I need to hear the facts of what Christ did at the cross. I need to hear that the price has been paid, but that healing can never seep into the deep places if it is not prepared in love and mercy. It needs to be tastefully done.

It was the people who loved me when I was unlovable and were there for me when nobody else was, who found a way into my soul. They sat with my questions and insecurities. They didn't label or judge me or try to prove me wrong. They asked the right questions to help me get to the heart of the matter. They trusted the Holy Spirit to bring conviction and perspective, and when they spoke the same words of correction in His assigned time, the words trickled deep into the hardest places of my heart and changed me from the inside out.

You see, you and I are the sous-chefs, and our lives are what is on the menu. How we live, how we speak, how we listen, is all being taken in by friends, family, and neighbors. Do we walk in the humility of knowing our own need for the gospel first and foremost? If we speak with conviction but fail to show our need to own up to the same truth, most people will not take the time to listen further, and we have done the gospel a disservice by making it so hard to hear the life-giving solution.

Don't be overwhelmed by this picture. I'm not writing this so you will start analyzing every word that comes out of your mouth. You and I will make mistakes. It's a part of being human. But are we quick to repent? Do we want our lives to reflect Him better? Are we burdened by the lost in our families and communities? Does their sin pain us because we know ultimately they are at war with God?

It's our heart He is after. Are our hearts surrendered to dependence on God for our own daily bread first and foremost?

oversalted

The gospel is not just about others, it's about us. If we are, with sincerity, sharing our faith because we know just how good the message is, He can use that salt—even tainted by our imperfections—for His glory.

There are some of us who need to lay off on the salt shaker though. There are some of us who need to remember the strongest things we bring to the table are the authenticity of our examples and our listening ears.

What we say matters, but how we live our lives carries far more influence. Are we working out our faith with fear and trembling? Are we more concerned with being heard or with hearing others? Are we confessing our sins one to another? Are we laying down our rights and trusting God to fight for us? It's love that paves the way for hard principles to be digested. It's a listening ear that paves the way for healing. It is a gracious spirit that is sensitive to the background and needs of our audience that gets truth across.

Quick side-note on love: A whole book could be written on the definition of love. Unfortunately, Merriam-Webster's definition does not do it justice. *Love* is defined as "a feeling of strong or constant affection for a person."[1] This does not even begin to scratch the surface of the meaning. We all know how fickle feelings can be. Love is so much bigger than that, as 1 Corinthians 13: 4-8 covers in detail. For the purposes of this book, let's look at one specific facet of love often overlooked in verse 6: "It does not rejoice at wrongdoing, but rejoices with the truth" (1 Corinthians 13:6, ESV).

Truth seeks to be honest about the gaping needs in our souls. The gospel states that we have deeply erred, and then declares with victory that we have been forgiven. Love acknowledges our lack and, far more importantly, the finished work of the cross in our stead. Our job is to present the truth in a way that is digestible to those who absolutely need the nutrition. That requires the proper use and seasoning of salt.

How to Properly Use Salt

The final prompt in Colossians 4 reminds us to know how to answer each person. We are each made uniquely. When you talk to your grandmother, I'm sure you start up the conversation thinking of her interests and generational expectations. You don't douse her with pop culture references and then remind her to text you on Snapchat or send you a TikTok. No; you talk to her about things that pertain to her. You speak to her from a standpoint she would understand. This is how every healthy relationship works, though some of us think every relationship should revolve around personal favorite topics. Knowing how to answer each person means we get to know what makes them tick. We speak to them from their take on the world, not ours.

I have learned to change my frame of reference based on my audience. One of my best friends recently had a huge breakthrough in her relationship with her in-laws, and it came from listening for the Holy Spirit's prompts to reign first and foremost. Because of her and her mother-in-law's different approaches to parenting, there had been a growing divide and hostility between the two of

oversalted

them. The Lord prompted her and her husband to begin praying about a Christmas trip to visit them.

When the trip came around, the Lord reminded her there was a bigger picture going on than that of her convictions about standards for her kids, so when a glass of Baileys Irish cream was offered early on Christmas morning, she sensed the Holy Spirit prompt her not to make it an issue. In fact, He prompted her to accept a glass and move on. There was something bigger afoot here than her personal preference.

Later, before lunch had been served, she was offered a glass of wine. She took that too. She barely drank them, but something about her accepting and holding the glasses changed the environment between her and her in-laws. Some type of protective shield came down in their midst, and following their trip, she and her husband received several phone calls asking them to come visit again; something that had not happened in the four years since she had started having kids.

This may seem minor, but for those of us who have a Pharisaical background or know too well the fundamentalist movement of the 80s and 90s, this is groundbreaking stuff. God is okay with you loving others in the way that seems comfortable to them. This is not sin. This is called winning people for the kingdom, and this is what discipleship and knowing how to answer others is about.

Sometimes, we Christians make mountains out of molehills. Alcohol is one of my favorite topics for this. I came from a dry college campus (which means there was no drinking of any kind).

First of all, making something a rule makes the desire to drink so much bigger than the issue itself. Secondly, Jesus' first public miracle was turning water into wine. Guys, Jesus' first public supernatural manifestation of His deity was to give wine at a celebration! Just because it has been misused does not mean we put a big fat X on it. Nor do we judge others who partake.

Romans 14 speaks to the different convictions of different believers, and in essence, tells us to drop frivolous and divisive debate. We are called to win souls. We each will give an account for our lifestyles and choices, and Jesus, the holiest of any judge, will call the verdict, so we don't need to do His job. We need to walk in obedience to the path and the call He has placed on us. And one thing I know He has called every one of us to do is love one another. Love, while it speaks truth, is wrapped in grace and mercy and seeks ultimately the unity of all believers.

∞

The issue here is not doctrine. It's not preferences or worldview. The point at stake is the gospel of Jesus Christ–the certainty that Jesus came, while we were still sinners, and died for us on that rugged cross; the testimony that He came to set us free, no longer to be subject to a yoke of slavery (Galatians 5:1, NASB, paraphrased). If we get caught up in petty squabbles, personal preferences, and our own misguided take on the world, we will miss out on the wonder of laying down our ways and embracing His better ones. If we work on our time frame instead of waiting for the Holy Spirit's prompts, then His life is not breathed into our words, and it is nothing but empty jargon and theology.

Oversalting, in essence, is the sin of legalism, where we have moved from being servants to judges. We step out of God's timing and do things without the lead of the Holy Spirit. It's the offense of the Pharisees, who knew every word of the law and yet missed out on the one who wrote it and came to fulfill it. We are called to be agents of healing in the world. We don't need another God. We've got one. He's bigger than our minds can even begin to comprehend. He made every culture, every tribe and every race, and He is the God of both truth and mercy wrapped into one. He is calling us to submit to getting to know Him and to learn how to be people who properly use salt.

There is a delicious salad waiting to be served. It's full of the nutrients that transformation and breakthrough are rooted in, and it has the power to deliver and heal every single time we step into communication with others. We need to be ready to serve that mélange in a palatable way so our guests might partake in the deep freedom of salvation. If we continue to over season the dish, those hungry for breakthrough will never get to taste the freedom underneath. I know I don't want to miss out on being a part of other people's healing, and we will, if we try to be master chefs and do things our way.

Some of us have been eating so much salt that we have forgotten the beauty of balance in our cooking. Jesus is calling

live out love

us out of trying to fix people our way and asking us to let Him be God. Let's be people who create space for God to do what we can't.

2

The three most POWERFUL WORDS

You Are Loved.

At the beginning of 2017, I hit my lowest place ever. I was still recovering from the fog of my second child's birth and the exhaustion from not sleeping soundly for over a year (Sleep deprivation is arguably one of the cruelest forms of torture known to man). My husband and I were ready to call it quits. Our home had become a toxic place full of frustration and misunderstandings. Every interaction was painful. It was so hard to see the light at the end of the tunnel.

I sought counselors, I read books, I psycho-evaluated myself and what I was doing wrong. But I repeatedly kept hitting a wall. I couldn't measure up. I kept failing. It was disillusioning and discouraging to say the least.

One of the hardest parts of my journey early on was that some of the people I sought out for counsel ended up making me feel even worse. They reminded me of my sin and where I had failed. Instead of first sitting with me and understanding my heart before trying to help me, they labeled me as "overly emotional," "preachy," and "too religious" (These were all true if we focus on the broken/human side of my spiritual giftings, but not spoken with a full understanding of the facts, in love or when I needed it). And after labeling, they tried to pour their version of a fix on me.

Please don't misunderstand; we absolutely need input from others. But we must be careful to find people who are for us; people who see the imprint of God on our lives and know how to call it out instead of making us feel like failures by focusing on where we lack. When our goal is simply fixing people and not actually caring about who they are as individuals, the results will always be rotten fruit.

I felt this so acutely watching the recent ROC Olympian and gold medal favorite, Kamila Valieva, come off the ice at the Beijing 2022 Olympics. Just days before the ladies' event that she was expected to win, news broke that the 15-year-old had tested positive for a banned substance at her Russian qualifiers several months earlier. Olympic pressure is already a lot for a teenager, but now there was swirling controversy around her. One of the most prolific and powerful skaters found herself falling repeatedly. It was so hard to watch her heightened emotions play out on the ice and her frustration with herself for failing to miss the mark she had sacrificed so much for and dedicated so many hours to.

What really broke me was when she got off the ice. Clearly

the three most powerful words

upset and disappointed in herself, the first thing her coach whispered to her in Russian was, "Why did you give up?" Even the commentators after the event continued to gape at just how coldly the immediate response had been from her team. In my mind, this was someone who just needed to know that she was enough; that she had worth greater than a medal. Instead, in a moment when her soul needed to breathe, she was surrounded by people telling her what she already knew. As she broke down in the score area, US commentator, Tara Lipinski, mentioned that someone just needed to hug that young woman.

Every human being has several innate needs. Two that must be met in order to experience healing are the desire to be known and the desire to be loved. Until those two are met, we are unable to process all of the stuff we need to grow and change. Knowing someone is for us is paramount to being able to receive feedback from them. As someone who has desperately needed metamorphosis in my life, I only started finding freedom and experiencing a breakthrough when I accepted just how valuable I was. Once I understood I was loved, healing started to happen, and change suddenly found its way into the parts of my life that needed transformation. Change starts first with identity; knowing not only who you are, but Whose you are.

I am No Victim

Before you can receive the truth of who you are, many of us have to first unlearn the lies. Understanding our identity is at the core of the human struggle. The enemy knows we were made in the image of God, and therefore next to destroying God's name, his number one goal is to cause you to question who you were created to be or pervert it. He does this through the lies spoken about us through others, and those we speak over our own lives.

Words have power. Scripture says that life and death are in the "power of our tongue" (Proverbs 18:21, ESV, paraphrased). Words spoken over us can and do stick. The words we speak and think over ourselves have the same effect. According to cognitive neuroscientist Dr. Caroline Leaf's[2] research, thoughts actually create matter in our brain. In photographs of the brain, you can actually see what the mind looks like after years of feeding itself toxic thoughts. In these images, the negative thoughts look like black twisted trees or a spreading poison. What are we feeding our minds on a daily basis?

Some of us may have been blessed to live around healthy human relationships, not experiencing the negative effects of toxic thinking. If you have found a circle that is life-giving in thought and words, thank God for those people, and make sure you also continue to be one of those people. When you start experiencing the dynamics of living in circles that do not breathe life or speak of hope, it's amazing how quickly the mind shrinks and the possibilities for hope shut down. The old mantra is true: you become like those you are around. So be wise about who you allow into the heart places.

I hadn't realized how many negative thinkers I had around me. People gave me lists of things I needed to do to experience a breakthrough in my marriage. They gave me rules to follow.

the three most powerful words

They told me what I was doing wrong and why I needed to repent. All were true, but I felt like I was drowning in truth. The truth of my sin—not the truth of the hope of the gospel. I find the Church often does this when we don't fully understand the importance of grace. This is why the various members of the Body need each other. It helps give us a robust picture of the gospel and who our God actually is.

It wasn't until I started speaking His truth over my life that something started to change in me. Music was one of the biggest ways I experienced a breakthrough in understanding my identity. Bethel's Kristine DeMarco's song "*I Am No Victim*" was life itself. I played it morning, noon, and night, as I wrestled with my identity. She reminded me that I was not a victim because of whose image I was made in. He is my Father who has good plans for me. I don't have to wonder if He will come through because He will. The same God who told a fearful and unbelieving Gideon in Judges 7:7, "I will save you," is the same God who has promised His faithfulness to you and me. Once He has said it, it's a done deal. God is unable to go back on His word. He is true to the very core of His being. "If we are faithless, he remains faithful, for he cannot disown himself" (2 Timothy 2:13, NIV).

When we declare the truth of who we are, it breaks something in the spiritual realm. It tells the voice of condemnation and accusation that we are actually beloved sons and daughters being molded more into our Father's image. We aren't failures. We are works in progress. When we tell the enemy of our soul that his lies no longer have power over us, suddenly the negative thoughts growing in our mind are combated by the truth of the character of our God. He is for me, not against me, and His plans for me will be accomplished (Jeremiah 29:11, NIV, paraphrased). This is foundational stuff for healing.

If you don't already have a system for declaring truth over your life, I encourage you to put this book down right now and create a system. My system is index cards on a key ring. Put a single hole punch and some extra blank cards on there, and every time you hear a verse that you know the Lord is declaring over you, write it down! If you don't know where to start, I recommend Jeremiah 29:11. Then put that somewhere you can see it, and speak it over yourself daily. You are loved and seen and known by the one who put the stars in the universe. Take a pause right now, and let that sink in. Then go grab those notecards.

Your True Identity

Did you know you are loved more deeply than you can even begin to imagine? Identity is key to properly understanding yourself—knowing not only who you are, but Whose you are. When I was growing up, it was all about girl power and the rise of female self empowerment. This is not what I'm talking about when I speak about identity. Any movement that seeks to self inflate without recognizing our brokenness and need for God is just another one of the world's antidotes to fill the God void. Walking in your God given identity is not about self promotion, which does not produce long-lasting freedom or change. We will

the three most powerful words

never be enough and therefore will always come up feeling empty because outside of Him and our need for Him, our weakness always comes to the surface.

The new twist on identity that this generation is wrestling with is one where all boundaries are thrown to the wind. We can now be whoever we want to be. We each find our own truth, the one that makes us feel good. But this twisting of truth will leave us feeling even more empty and confused, as we realize we can never change enough to fix our need for God. The truth is, we can't work hard enough or change enough to be enough. We will fail, and we will see our lack because we were never intended to be enough on our own.

Did you know there is someone who has seen the full extent of your brokenness and imperfections? He saw it all, and still, He came for you. And the good news is, He is not going to stop coming for you.

When you are in a season of struggle, human nature's response is to pull back and selfishly buffer. I am convinced this is where "ice cream therapy" after a break-up comes from. You try to self-soothe, since needs aren't being met. If we find our identity in a relationship, and the feelings are not reciprocated, this can devastate us. I utilized this numbing technique for years during my twenties, via social outings with friends and lots of chick flicks late at night, but thanks to the wise writing of women like Priscilla Shirer, Jess Connelly, Lara Casey Isaacson, and Kim Hyland, I began to realize my worth was entirely established at the cross. In fact, God solidified this truth through the gorgeous song "*Known,*" written by the anointed Tauren Wells. It defined the transformation of my soul in 2018, as God spoke over me my true identity in Him. I had been insecure and trying to prove my worth most of my life, and the Lover of my soul gently told me: it was already finished. He chose me. He saw my worth. And that was all I needed.

The chorus reminds us: We are fully known—He sees even the deepest, darkest and worst stuff you hide from the world; even the stuff our significant other and parents can't stomach. Yet, in the midst of that full disclosure of brokenness, here is the good news of it all: we are fully loved—unconditionally and wildly by Him. We can grasp the hard truth of Him knowing our yuck, while also dancing freely in the incredible grace of His undeserved gift. From this position, we are suddenly equipped to do what we were called to do.

When I realized I was loved by the Creator of the heavens and the earth with an unrelenting love that would not stop pursuing me until He had captured every part of my heart and soul, I found unexplainable peace and security. The fog lifted, and I was able to become the wife my husband needed in the places he was struggling.

When our basic human need of knowing we are known is met, anything can happen.

My prayer for you, reader, first and foremost, is you would find your true identity in the broken and hard-to-love places. That's what He came for. He came for you in those messy places, to let you know just how beloved and cherished you are. Your

the three most powerful words

identity is the one He placed in you. It doesn't have a title. It's not affiliated with a certain company or brand. It's not found in the family you were born into or your nationality or financial status. It's simply you. You and all your quirks. You and all your scars. Who you are in the presence of your King is who you really are.

If you are realizing there are still areas where you believe falsehoods about yourself, you don't have to sweat it. Those are mindsets that are still being sanctified. You don't have to fix it all, in yourself or in others. He's got it. "He who began a good work in you will bring it to completion on the day of Jesus Christ" (Philippians 1:6, ESV). And He will do it in His perfect timing, as we slowly submit to the process of the Refiner. As the "*Reckless Love*" anthem, by Cory Asbury reminded me in my dark season, there is no shadow or mountain that He won't move when coming after you. He will redeem and restore and refine you. It won't be easy or what you prefer, but He will slowly help you look more like His Son (who loves you exactly where you are, even as He is helping refine you to be more like Him).

The Kiss Tank

Identity is critical in understanding our value. It keeps us from responding with defensiveness when people point out directly or inadvertently our weaknesses and failures. Once we know who we are, we can step into a place of ministry to those around us who are hurting. Instead of taking the bait of their unkindness and gossip, we can start viewing them from a lens of being made in the image of Christ and in need of His love and forgiveness. Most people who are unkind with their words are usually hurting deeply and simply expressing that pain by attempting to push that pain on others.

My daughter and I have started this new tradition of gassing up her love tank. Just like my car needs fuel to run, our kids' little hearts need love to function well, so sometimes she comes and parks herself at our dining room table and tells me she is ready for a fill up in her kiss tank. Then I eat her up with kisses until she is "full," and she runs around saying "My love tank is full." It's adorable, to say the least, and a physical reminder to me that knowing we are loved is required before we are ready to hear the hard stuff.

My background and human tendency, as I mentioned before, is to correct the wrong thinking and actions immediately to get my daughter to "behave." The truth is, we can work on someone's actions as much as we want, but if the heart remains unchanged, then we accomplish nothing.

I was raised in the Christian subculture where immediate obedience was something that was emphasized. I agree this is a healthy standard to uphold, as we do want our children to understand that the world does not wait for them to get around to following the rules. It is Biblical to teach obedience so that our kids understand the importance of walking in submission to the Lord. That being said, in many areas of my life I obeyed with my actions, but my heart was not engaged. As an adult, I'm grateful for when my dad took the time to talk me through issues when I was seething; when he met my rebellious heart

the three most powerful words

with kindness and mercy. Knowing I was loved by him softened the soil of my heart to help me change and do the right thing, not to check a box and move on. I obeyed because I desired to do it. It was his love that paved a way for me to step into obeying.

I've seen the same things in my daughter's heart. I've watched her bristle and the animosity in our home increase as I forced my parental rules on her. I've also watched her switch when I started the conversation by first reminding her that she is completely loved by her mother no matter what. When I start my convos by reminding her of her identity—"You are precious to me. There is a call on your life. There is no one like you."—it changes my interactions with her. When I remind her that she is loved, it softens her heart, and she becomes extremely flexible to growth, discipline, and doing what's right. In fact, when we have any form of discipline, I communicate to her that I hate doing it, but there is a price to be paid when we do things wrong. I remind her through every single consequence that I love her so much, and nothing will ever change that. I discipline her because I love her heart too much to let her stay in her sin.

Discipline moments are in fact occasions to remind our children of how loved they are. Recently, I have taken to asking her to please stop disobeying because I do not enjoy disciplining her at all: "Please obey, so Mom doesn't have to do this thing that hurts her heart." It really clicked for her in our last discussion. She gets that I don't like to do this. She gets that I am doing it because I love her too much to let her stay in her selfishness.

Some of the best lessons I have ever learned were in observing what created room for growth and change in my heart, and then learning to apply those personal lessons to the way I interact with other people. My brain may tell me one thing, but proof is in the pudding.

Where does change stem from? What is the ingredient that has transformed lives throughout history? What can we learn from the lives lived around us? If we could exercise a little humility and listen, we would realize transformation does not begin with human logic, but heavenly wisdom. Jesus gave His life for a sinful and rebellious people. Even as He is holy, He is also merciful. It's love that prepares the way for the lessons to be learned. Love paves the way for hard truth to be digested in deep places.

You may desperately want to give that child of yours a talking to or remind your spouse of what they are called to do, but learn from my years of mistakes; this only creates a wall between you and them. What if you simply told them: "You are heard, and you matter." Can you imagine the difference that would make in their life?

We may know all the right things to say to change the people in our life, but the one thing I have learned over and over is this: intellectual arguments don't win hearts. The three most powerful words you can ever tell someone are, "You are loved." Then step back and watch God do His thing.

3

The heart
BEHIND IT ALL

> My dear brothers and sisters, take note of this:
> Everyone should be quick to listen,
> slow to speak and slow to become angry.
> James 1:19, NIV

We stand at a crossroads in the American Christian Church. Culture is pushing for tolerance. And while there is no freedom when we ignore our sin, there is a heart cry coming in the midst of the cultural shift, one that we would be wise to tune into. If we only "die on our hills" and push in the opposite direction of culture, we will do more harm than good. We aren't called to just be pillars of truth, but also ambassadors of hope and healing. I believe, in the midst of this call for tolerance, there is actually a longing for grace, for a re-focusing reminder of a Father who came and loved us while we were still sinners. If we don't stop and listen to the heart, I believe we will miss an opportunity. We win souls through our love paired with truth.

I think a lot of us on our soapboxes forget a hugely important Biblical fact: Jesus does not need us to fight for His name's sake.

He is plenty powerful enough to flood the entire Earth and send fire down on a city if need be. No; He doesn't need us to prove Him or fight for His glory. He's got that.

What He needs us to do is reflect Him by standing on His truth, while walking in His steps. Jesus called out the woman at the well and the woman caught in adultery, but He did it in a way that wrapped them in the love they always desired. He told them He saw them in all of their filth and guilt, and that He had prepared a way to wash them as white as snow.

The young people of our culture are crying out for someone to hear their hearts, for someone to hear the "why" behind their drug addiction, porn obsession, and repetitive broken relationship patterns. The truth is, most don't want those lifestyles. In fact, they feel trapped, and they are trying to fill a huge gaping hole that can only be filled by the Creator of the universe. If we could give them a taste of His heart, we could lead them to a well that will satisfy them forever.

The Messy Call to Discipleship

Our culture is looking for a Savior. That neighbor who doesn't come out of their home, the cashier who won't make eye contact, that person who cut you off in traffic; each is made in the image of God. Ecclesiastes reminds us that God "planted eternity" in the hearts of mankind (Ecclesiastes 3:11, NLS). The imprint of their Maker is there. St. Augustine writes in his Confessions that "Our hearts are restless until they rest in You."[3] This means every human is in search of the One for which they

the heart behind it all

were created.

We want people to come to us tidied up and without their issues. We want them to be forgiving and kind. We want them to not get angry or gossip. We want them to not be wrestling with sexual brokenness and living with baggage and consequences from a life lived in this fallen world. But here is a wake-up call the Body of Christ needs to hear: those longing to know Christ don't check the right "Christian boxes." They probably have some really broken ways of thinking. Maybe they don't even believe that sin is real. They may even believe they are basically good people. Discipleship and the work of sharing the gospel is messy and not cookie cutter. It's not about changing the outside, but the inside. The lies of the enemy run deep in those who don't know Him, and if the Church wants to be a part of setting people free, she has to be okay getting messy. She has to be okay hearing people's hearts and not always hearing what she wants to hear—knowing that God is big enough to sort through it all in His perfect time.

Our job is not to correct every piece of wrong thinking as we meet the unchurched or mischurched because we may miss out on the heart change that the Spirit of God is doing, one little piece at a time. Paul calls out the Church arguing over disputable matters of conscience and conviction. "Who are you to judge someone else's servant? To their own master, servants stand or fall. And they will stand, for the Lord is able to make them stand" (Romans 14:4, NIV).

Who are we to judge the journey the Lord has set our

neighbor on, or how He chooses to save and transform them? Are we their Creator? Our job is to obey His promptings of how we are to be ministers of truth and grace. We must listen to our Father's voice and obey because that is where the work of transformation takes place; not on our timeframe, but on His.

We get to be a part of this incredible work God is doing on Earth, but this requires that we live fearlessly and not play it safe because the wisdom of man holds no comparison to the power of God (1 Corinthians 2:5, NIV). We have to give up our versions of how things should look and how we think God should work. Instead, we put our faith in a God who is bigger than us and is redeeming all things for His glory. He's got us. He's got them. He is doing His thing. We don't have to play God because He has had that role for generations, and He hasn't failed anyone yet.

When to Talk and When to Listen

We tend to line up on one end of the spectrum or the other; don't we? We either are direct and unashamed about sharing what people need to change way too early, or we just listen and listen and listen and let people stay trapped in their pain. Oh, how our culture needs relationships that know how to do the dance–the listening, the relationship building, the loving, and then pairing that with God-led, Holy Spirit-inspired, convincing truth. Our words have nothing to give if the Holy Spirit doesn't breathe life into another's heart.

Our modern day culture seems to lean towards letting

the heart behind it all

listening and love win the day, so I will spend more time identifying what it means to listen appropriately, and also (very importantly), what it does not mean.

Following the most recent high profile royal British wedding, I was privy to an online debate over the new Duchess of Sussex, Meghan Markle's, history and how church leaders are feeling led to call her out because of her past sin (aka divorce). I was frustrated to say the least. Here were people of God who had no relationship with her and no direct connection to her story (where she is now or how she got there), giving their opinion on the situation. This is what it is not supposed to look like. There was no relationship, no love, and no one is set free by the words uttered. The Lord is not honored in this way. We have no idea who might be reading those words and how they might be received.

How many women might have walked through the pain of an unwanted divorce (fighting to remain sometimes in the face of abuse)? This is not what speaking the truth looks like. There are people who have closed up and walked out on the Church because of words spoken thoughtlessly and without grace; words that hit pain points in people without considering the full weight of their heartbreak. We would be wise to think before we spoke.

So you might be asking what about vulnerability and honesty? Where is the space to be able to just speak and share the thoughts we are wrestling through where our theology and reality don't match up? Many of us don't have healthy safe circles to share and do life with. Facebook and social media have become the place where we take free reign to share our personal

live out love

perspective and opinions to whoever takes the time to read, whether or not they are in a place to receive. Maybe you do have a tight-knit friend or family circle you call or who calls you to share the places where they are wrestling through frustration or confusion. We all need that.

Vulnerability is powerful. It gives our soul a place to breathe and can be an opportunity for untruths to be revealed and dismantled. Sharing our heart helps us process our wrong thinking and to be seen and heard. But sharing our frustrations with someone who agrees with us and digging down deeper into our way of thinking is dangerous. We must not be friends who just vent or make space for others to vent but don't want to hear feedback or a perspective that challenges us to think differently. We must ask ourselves, to what end we vent? Is it to find someone who'll commiserate with our sinful heart? Is it to be real and seen? Unleashing the evil of our heart and wanting to hear none of His truth in return should not be practiced.

When I have those friends wanting to share their heart (unloading their pain), my job is to listen. My job is to love. My job is to pray for a word from God to speak into their lives. When people are in pain, all of their misconceptions come spilling out. All of the lies we believe are right there for the picking. As a truth lover myself, I have found it hard not to jump in right at that moment to try to tweak and redirect to His truth.

While the heart behind this is admirable, we confuse the "power of man" and the "power of God" and miss out on divine opportunities for freedom. It's in these moments that

the heart behind it all

the people of God need to learn to listen for His voice and His timing. The enemy wants us to jump in too soon and out of alignment with the Holy Spirit's leading, and those who are vulnerably sharing their hearts with us will quickly shut up shop. The heart builds a wall, and the truth never gets to touch the places that are crying out for it.

Friends, when I'm dying in my sin, when I want to hear someone speak truth to my soul, the first thing I need to know is: Do they love me? Do they really care about my heart? Do they hear me? Once that is established, then the heart is ready to receive.

You see; it's the words that correspond with the work of the Spirit that give life. Usually the people who spoke truth to me—the kind of truth that ignites my heart to change and repent—had no idea they had any part in the process. They were simply loving and living; God divinely lined up their words with where my heart was, to show me His kindness and love for me.

What are the words that speak life? Words of validation create trust. "I feel you. I hear you." Those words mean a lot. They help build emotional connection. They build a bridge for truth to be planted later on. They may not unlock doors, but they set the groundwork for His Word which can.

We do need to clarify that there is no amount of empathy that will help redirect someone's path. Those who are always "identifying" with others' struggles and standing by their friends and family (even in their sin), can lead those they love into further bondage by failing to speak truth. We must be careful to not lean too far towards just being a listening ear.

On the other end of the spectrum, there is no amount of truth that can set free someone who is wounded. True care and friendship is critical for trust and truth that sets free. As Proverbs reminds us, "Wounds from a friend can be trusted, but an enemy multiplies kisses" (Proverbs 27:6, NIV). When a friend speaks God's truth wrapped in unconditional love that speaks to my sin and their desire to see me set free, that changes everything! Jess Connelly calls it "a calling up," instead of just calling out.[4] We are called to be sisters and brothers who speak life at the right moment. Let's be believers willing to sit with the Lord before speaking; to seek His voice for hard situations in others' lives. Let's be people who listen and wait on His lead because He alone has the answer.

Creating Safe Places

So how do we learn to become facilitators who truly love one another enough to communicate in a way that actually creates change? This process is often far from simple and will require that we do some deep self reflection through the process of laying down our preferences and opinions about what others should do and look like.

Let me introduce you to my friend Alison (name changed for the purposes of her privacy and this book). Alison was raised in a Christian family which loved her well. She was also the victim of molestation from a pedophile at a young age. She figured out how to separate that place of pain in her mind, and she moved on and

the heart behind it all

lived an "okay" life. But she never dealt with the heart wounds, and she was extremely bitter at the fact that her perpetrator was never brought to justice. She continued to cover up the scars with abusive relationships, and eventually she moved on to drugs and alcohol to numb herself. She didn't dress like a Christian girl and people in the Church often gave her a look when she came looking for help and belonging. She didn't feel worthy of finding healing and wholeness. Her body was working overtime to protect her soul via selective memory. When someone has gone through trauma, the body tells the mind to minimize or forget because the memory of experience puts so much stress on the functioning of our body. The mind/body/soul connection is so much deeper than we can even begin to realize.

Her journey to healing began with mindful meditation and creating space to process her pain. As she began to accumulate tools to overcome in her story, she wanted to help others to find freedom from similar traumas. It was in that process, being trained to teach, that she realized how many layers in herself still needed to be dealt with. You can't give what you don't have. She couldn't just heal her body. She also had to heal her soul and spirit.

Who helped her? What was the catalyst to her finding wholeness? Was it someone who judged her for her promiscuous appearance and numbing lifestyle choices? She met those. Was it someone who questioned why she kept that secret for so long? Was it someone who pitied her and her victimization? No; she met a friend who created a safe place for her to be real about her brokenness and her struggles. She found someone who was for her, and suddenly, the things kept in the dark places found the light. God started working the deep healing in her that only He can.

As she found a safe place to process the deep wounds and broken thought patterns, she slowly opened up and stepped into more Biblically sound teaching. She now co-runs an incredible Christian business based out of Australia that is helping women find freedom from trauma. The brand is growing and expanding internationally. And it all started because one person took the time to listen, love, and create space for the Holy Spirit to do the deep work.

∽

Transformation starts with a heart change in us. Healing is found in a posture of surrender before the King, when we create space to let Him use us as He sees fit. It has nothing to do with our ideas, our vision, or our trying to fix the world. Breakthrough has everything to do with His plan of redemptive work. The Holy Spirit is the heartbeat of God moving in power on the earth.

Have you ever had that sense deep in your spirit that the Lord just worked through you? There was something about the words that came out of your mouth that you knew didn't come from your own thought process. That's what we need to be waiting on: those unmistakable promptings of peace. That's where we need to rest, being patient for His timing.

I pray we would hear these words and become women who speak freedom and life to our friends. Let's be people who make

the heart behind it all

the difficult truth pill easier to swallow.

Having been close at one time doesn't give us the right, as Jess Connelly reminds us in her recent book, *Dance Stand Run.* We have to earn the right to talk.[5] This applies to our kids and spouses as well.

No investment; no return. Even if we both mutually want it, the heart won't allow for truth without a relationship. Trust must be built first. The mind/body/soul connection is God-given. I've heard it said that rules without relationship breed rebellion. How true that is! Life-giving words require relationship. We need someone who has walked through our daily valleys, cried with us in hard moments, and shared their own struggles as well.

Trust takes time to develop. We have to be patient. Most importantly, we need to be pressed into His presence. It's from personal and unseen intimacy with the Father that we will better know His heart for a circumstance, and from that place alone, true healing will flow into others' lives. He knows the right moment to remove that tumor and sew up the incision of the soul. He will give us words. He will prompt because it's the Spirit alone who can do the hard heart work.

Our words are hollow, empty, and without power, but the Spirit of God– one can not contain His strength, His hope, and His ability. Be a friend who allows that type of power to flow in and through you. Be a taste of heaven's sweet revival.

4
Just one piece
OF THE PUZZLE

> Just as a body, though one, has
> many parts, but all its many parts
> form one body, so it is with Christ.
> 1 Corinthians 12:12, NIV

My daughter was calling out to me from the kitchen as I prepared dinner. "Mom, come help me with this puzzle. I don't know where this piece goes. Where does this go? Come help me." I responded, with my hands dripping in enchilada sauce, "What does the box say? Do you see the picture? Where do you think that piece goes?" Part of being a parent is helping your child grow slowly into independence (and you being able to finish making dinner in a timely way).

My daughter was trying to put together a 100-piece puzzle without knowing what the final picture looked like. She was guessing. The pieces were tiny, and to her four-year-old brain, the job was enormous. How was she supposed to put this entire thing together?

live out love

Without the picture of the puzzle, we all are clueless regarding the final masterpiece; aren't we? The more complicated the puzzle, the more likely we will not be able to put it together without some sort of roadmap.

How many of us attempt to do life like this? Or church? We have our piece, and everyone else needs to fit in with what we see.

Oh, foolish little puzzle piece. You are but one piece, and even if you are a center piece, you have at least four other pieces that connect to you. Without the other pieces, you don't know how the hundreds (or maybe thousands) of others intersect with you. You have to be able to scale way back and see the full picture.

How many of us, like my four-year-old, are trying to force pieces that don't fit into our mold, attempting to make the picture work according to our vision? What a messed up picture we would get, and with too many wasted pieces on the side.

We will talk about Saul (the first King of Israel) deeper in chapter 6, "Get Out of the Way." After the Spirit of God left him, and David was anointed as the new king, Saul began to grow jealous and fearful of David. He saw the presence of God moving in and through him, and he feared something he couldn't control.

How often have church leaders failed to be flexible and allow growth and the work of God in their midst because they got caught up in how God used to work? Being comfortable and worshiping yesterday's manna is a prevalent sin I have seen far too many Christian leaders fall prey to. They have their eyes fixed on their accomplishments of the past. But behold; He is the God who does new work.

just one piece of the puzzle

I have heard it said that the Kingdom of God is a place where birthing happens. Leaders should be cultivating other leaders. There should be a newness of God's presence and plans being birthed in seasons. When spring comes, we know it because flowers begin to bloom. In the same way, the fruit should be apparent in our lives and churches. If God's plans are being brought to earth, there will be lost coming to Christ in our congregations. We will see lives being transformed and being made into His image. I'm so grateful to be a part of a Church that loves well. We don't judge people for their sexual choices, for example. We preach the Word of God, but we don't hyper focus on issues. We wait to see what the Holy Spirit is doing.

I have had testimonies come in through our college programs around the country of students changing their sexual identity to their God-given design because they were loved so well by the Body of Christ. Partnered with the discipleship and love of a Church that knows how to walk in step with God, His Word did the convicting. That's what it's supposed to look like. Both young believers and old believers need to be growing deeper in sanctification and being made more like Christ. The fruit will be apparent. The newness of Christ will be at work.

The fruit of something different than what the world offers must be apparent and changing and increasing in our midst. This is the newness I speak of. There must be a humble flexibility to be busy about the Lord's new work instead of focusing on the old thing. I've been in churches that spoke fondly of the Lord's work in past seasons but forgot to change with Him as a new season approached.

We have to stay in lockstep with Him. There must be a utilization of the members and a pouring into the next generation, not a fear of it. These are signs of the Spirit of God at work in surrendered people.

A Cross-Cultural and Multi-Generational Body of Christ

We are but one tiny cog in the generational and cross-cultural body known as Christ's bride. I write to those who think God is only from one political party or perhaps from a country they know, or a socio-economic group they are comfortable with. We all just have one piece of the puzzle. We agree Jesus is "the way, the truth and the life," but when it comes to many controversial issues in the church: to drink or not to drink, baptism of infants, dance in the Church, words of prophecy, healing, etc., we each capture but a glimmer of eternity (John 14:6, NIV).

The other day I was asked what my theological background was, and I wasn't quite sure how to answer. I don't fit into any box. I am a truth-seeking, charismatic-dancing, doxology-loving, Holy Spirit-believing, church history-admiring saint. I don't really have a tribe. I see the colors of my Lord in all these different branches of His people.

A little background: I was raised by a converted Catholic in a charismatic Bible church in Hawaii. I enjoyed rich times of fellowship in college, in a grace-focused community, while also attending a small Christian liberal arts college where "Calvinism vs. Arminianism" was hotly debated in the cafeteria hall. After graduating, I enjoyed vibrant worship and teaching in an Anglican church that fell under the African Episcopal Church.

just one piece of the puzzle

They had a strong theology, two hundred years of church history, and exuberant congregational worship. Anglicans who lift their hands? Yes! There has always been a tenuous balance in my life between seeking meaty theological truth and needing something real and charismatic that I can sink my passion into.

My friends come from many different streams of the Body. I have friends who understand the intricacies of theological truths and can defend the faith in ways that the analytical mind requires, while others proclaim Jesus best through their kindness and service. Then there are my fellow lioness sisters who break strongholds through the laying on of hands and praying in tongues. I have seen God do unthinkable things in their midst: delaying surgeries, casting out demons, and seeing people's health miraculously restored!

Most of the time my spectrum of friends don't fully understand or get along with one another, and honestly I don't always understand them fully either. I remember one birthday when I had my six closest girlfriends go to dinner, and I realized just how diverse and varied their perspectives on the world were. That is how the body of Christ is designed: dynamically diverse and different for a purpose. As 1 Corinthians 12, reminds us:

> If the whole body were an eye, where would the sense of hearing be? If the whole body were an ear, where would the sense of smell be? But in fact God has placed the parts in the body, every one of them, just as he wanted them to be. If they were all one part, where would the body be? As it is, there are many parts, but one body.
>
> 1 Corinthians 12: 17-20, NIV

live out love

The creativity of God is beyond limit. There are so many dimensions to God and to His world. It would make sense that the Body of Christ on our little Earth would be displayed in a variety of ways. The human body, for example, has variety and purpose and divine design woven into the fabric of each cell and system. Did you know the axon of the nervous system can not communicate with the rest of the central nervous system without a simple protective layer known as the myelin which protects and enhances its signal? Two very different parts function together as one to get the job done. The layers of God's creation are truly mind-boggling. The smartest of scientists are only beginning to scratch the surface of understanding.

And then there are the heavens! When you think about the vastness of space, the utter incomprehensibility of black holes, and inexplicable supernatural dimensions in the heavenly realms, there is a glory that we can not even begin to understand. Yet, in Jeremiah 33:3, He invites us to seek Him that we might learn the unsearchable things.

If the human body and the heavens have more variety and detail and dimension than we can explain or experience, then it would certainly make sense that the body of Christ would also show this type of varied creativity. To simplify, just as each of us have different friends that reflect different facets of our interests and personalities, so the different parts of Jesus' Church reflect different facets of our all-powerful, omnipresent, and glorious Savior.

Now before some people label me a heretic or extremist by mistakenly assuming that I lean towards a humanistic Christian worldview that says "There are many roads that lead to God," let me clarify: there is falseness out there. There is an enemy who seeks to confuse and pervert God's truth. There is a movement that seeks to experience God's power in worship and miracles without walking through the brokenness and repentance it requires to taste true breakthrough. There is a falseness clothed in light that seeks to push God's beautiful gift of love and grace at the expense of His Truth. They exclaim certain parts of His Word without mentally wrestling with other parts that would contradict their claims.

In essence, there are many who would seek to be their own gods and create their own comfortable truth. That's secular humanism, the belief in the potential value and goodness of human beings outside of Christ. Isn't that the oldest fight man has had with God since the Garden of Eden? To be like Him, knowing good and evil. Not needing Him. Being our own little gods. We may have given Humanism a name, but it's been a sin issue since the beginning.

If one good thing can be said to have come out of the modern day movement for diversity, it is the Church moving towards understanding that Jesus is more dynamic than we could even begin to imagine. His Word gives us a guidepost by which to discern who He is and find the Truth, for all "truths" are not His.

It is very short-sighted for any Christian to think they have the entire picture of who Christ is. When we think we have the full perspective, we can become stumbling blocks to those searching who don't fit into the mold we are operating in. Instead of being a catalyst for healing, we can become catalysts for confusion and more hurt. The more time I spend in His Word, the more I realize I have only begun to scratch the surface of who my awesome God is. I am but one little piece, and there are many players in God's grand plan. At the Anglican church we attended for a couple years, I remember one lady saying, "I'm just on the Anglican bus to Heaven." I loved that! She recognized the church she was thriving in was not the only way to experience Christ.

Let me clarify. Yes; Jesus is the only way. Let me specify that one unchanging eternal truth. There are false truths out there that seek to lead men astray from the God who can save and revive them, but there is also a falseness lurking in "religious" attire that seeks to puff up our pride and tell us that we know every dimension of our glorious King and that our way of practicing faith is the only way to Him. Just look at the Pharisees of Jesus' day, knowing the truth but not getting to experience it when they were standing face to face with the embodiment of the Word.

Perspective in Community

We were not created to be islands. We were created as parts of a whole.

I think there is a misconception about mission and ministry in our society; a belief that some are called to it and others are not. There is a belief that only certain personality types have the giftings to impact others–that you have to be on staff at a church to be important.

How much we miss with this mindset! Peter tells us, "But you are a chosen people, a royal priesthood, a holy nation, God's special possession, that you may declare the praises of him who called you

just one piece of the puzzle

out of darkness into his wonderful light" (1 Peter 2:9, NIV).

When we are changed by the blood of the Lamb, we get a new identity. We each have been called to the priesthood. Inside every single believer of Jesus Christ there is a call to be in relationship with others as members of the body of Christ. This is our most important role. You have been specifically gifted with unique talents for a purpose: to equip and inspire the lives you have been given stewardship over for the sake of the gospel.

What is true friendship about? It is not just about people who you enjoy being with, but your close-knit circle of friends who know you to your core and can help you become who you are called to be. These are friends who have proven they have your best interest at heart and understand that calling you higher is in your best interest.

I know I want relationships that help me to step into all God has called me to be. We weren't called to just be here to enjoy some good games and celebrate a couple holidays. We were created to point one another to His truth. We are called to equip believers through accountability and relationships empowered by the Holy Spirit. We are here to better serve His body so that the name of Jesus might be glorified throughout the earth. I believe discipleship at its heart is the facilitating of the gifts of others around us.

These relationships will be different at times. When one friend is hurting, we all have roles to play in their healing journey. If we were all exhorting her, can you imagine how trapped she might feel? But if one is encouraging, one exhorting, and another giving practical help, think how supported and strengthened that balance would be? For the giftings of those in His Body are as varied and diverse as He is. My husband and I have both a marriage counselor and a mentor couple in our life. Our counselor functions as an advocate and validator of the hard stuff we are wrestling through, and our mentors are more like parents calling out the sin in our lives. Between the two of them, we find the balance we need to be loved and transformed.

I'll never forget one of the most profound moments when the Lord made the diverse roles of the Body so crystal clear to me. A dear friend of mine had been wrestling with a spiritually mismatched marriage for years. Her pain grew to bitterness, and her husband responded with the only thing he knew from his own broken father's example: running into the arms of another woman. They remained husband and wife under the same roof while the pain festered in both their hearts.

I wrestled with my role in this relationship. I like to be a truth speaker. When she came to my house to share her hurts, I wanted to call her out on the areas where she was not loving her husband well by talking ill of him consistently (and there were certainly moments when I did bring that up). But I got a very strong sense from the Holy Spirit that my job in this relationship was to listen. When I thought about confronting her, His peace was not there.

My faith wavered many times. Would this situation always be as it was? Was anyone speaking the truth to her? I told one of my dear sisters in Christ, who was aware of the situation, that I didn't know if I needed to speak up and say the hard thing.

just one piece of the puzzle

The Holy Spirit didn't tell me to do this. I just wondered, in my strength, if I needed to, and my wise friend reminded me we each have a role. Do the thing He is asking you to do, and that will be enough.

I won't hide this from you. I got frustrated with the local church for not stepping in more. Isn't that what they are called to do? Then again, who is the Church? The person up on the pulpit? The Bible study leader? Or is there a role each and every one of us plays in God's Body? I am a part of the Church. You are the Church. Sometimes the person God is calling to step into an uncomfortable situation is you.

I'll never forget when we got that email. Her husband wanted to work on their marriage! She emailed seven women and told us she knew that God was calling her to obey. When I saw the names on that email, I realized there were seven of us speaking, listening, and loving in our different roles to her, and in the beauty of community, she heard the voice of the Lord calling her to walk in love and forgiveness. Now, more than five years later, they have welcomed the arrival of their third child—new life! Each of us had played our part, and God had done the deep heart work.

What if I had overstepped my role? What if I had not listened to the Holy Spirit, said what I'd wanted, and not given her a place for her heart and hurt to land? Would the Holy Spirit have had the room to do His work with me in the way?

We each have a part to play. We have to stop looking to others to step in when God has placed a situation before us. We need to humbly ask God, "What are You asking me to do here?" He will equip us, by His Spirit, for the task that He has specifically called us to. We don't need to take the friend across the finish line and make it all happen—we just need to obey His promptings.

The Value of Every Life

That brings me to the flip side. Though we can't take over the whole show, we cannot underestimate the importance of our role.

Have you ever seen the classic Jimmy Stewart movie, "It's a Wonderful Life"? It's my absolute favorite film of all time. It's the story of a man, George Bailey, who questions the meaning of his life after his bank has to file for bankruptcy. Long story short, he is a compassionate soul. As he looks at his life and the dreams he sacrificed for the sake of the people of Bedford Falls, he wonders to himself, "What do I have to show for myself?"

Have you ever been in this place? You've made sacrifices, put other people before yourself, and perhaps felt you still came up empty?

In a moment of desperation, George thinks everything is lost. His life has nothing to show for it, and he is stuck in the same town he always dreamed of escaping. He decides to end his life, but just as he attempts to, a strange little man appears and jumps off the bridge George was considering jumping off of. The compassionate side of George kicks into high gear, and he decides to jump into mission mode to help the stranger. This stranger turns out to be an angel who has come to show George just how valuable his life is. He then takes him on a journey of seeing what life would be like if he had never lived.

just one piece of the puzzle

The impact of every single life can not be underestimated. There are friends, family, neighbors who benefit from your unique makeup and giftings. Is there someone you have listened to recently? Spoken a word of encouragement to? Picked up? Dropped off? Sent a note/card to? Said hello to? Do not underestimate the power of those little acts of kindness. Do not underestimate the coincidental connections of backgrounds, giftings, and interests of people who live next door to you or you keep running into randomly.

I call those divine interventions. God is sovereignly showing you He is a part of writing and weaving this incredible story of your life. Ephesians reminds us that, "We are His workmanship, created in Christ Jesus for good works, which God prepared beforehand, that we should walk in them" (Ephesians 2:10, ESV).

We can't write ourselves out of His plan. There aren't some of us called and some of us not. If you were made in His image, and you are living and breathing, then you are called on. So stop making excuses about how you're "not as gifted as so and so" or how you don't have some other skill set that he or she has. We have to stop giving up our birthright as sons and daughters of the King. We each have unique giftings, backgrounds, and stories. And there is purpose in all of it.

Make no mistake; the trials you've been journeying through are not a fluke. Your neighbors—not a coincidence. Your co-workers—strategically placed around you by God. We each have been given a unique community of people who God has strategically placed us in for a purpose greater than ourselves. Your unique struggles, He can use to set other people free!

This is what we have been called to do. We're called to make an impact: to help others step into their God-given potential. I love a quote from Lara Casey: "Jesus didn't have a megaphone or an Instagram account or even a car. He had two feet and one goal. Little by little, person by person, He changed all of history."[6]

God needs your unique flavor to impact this world. Each and every one of us has immense influence in the Kingdom of God. It starts with our spouses and our kids, and then extends to our neighbors and communities. One prayer group I used to meet with called it our "oikos map." Oikos is Greek for "household." If you look at the early Church, the gospel was spread through relational networks. Our unique flavor impacts first the people who we live with intimately. Each of those lives directly impact other lives, and the map grows.

Who has God placed in your path this week that you can serve? Who has God put right in front of you that could use your love and encouragement? Are we helping others step into their God-designed roles in the Body of Christ by living out our walk with integrity?

You are a leader, friend. You are called to discipleship. When you start running in the mission He has set before you, this world gets set on fire! I don't know about you, but that's the kind of world I want to live in—one where every human being is living up to their God-given potential. If we would just step up and do our part, God will do the rest. He's got the master picture, and He's waiting for you to play your part and put your piece into place.

5

Work of
THE SPIRIT

If the sin of the Old Testament times was the rejection of God the Father,
and the sin of the New Testament times was the rejection of God the Son,
then the sin of our times is the rejection of God the Holy Spirit.
Dr. Stephen and David Olfrod[7]

I grew up in a Bible church, but one layered in Pacific island culture, history, and lots of "Aloha." The music in Hawaii, and in the church I was raised in particularly, was powerful: anointed, soul-satisfying, and fulfilling.

When I turned eighteen, I moved to the east coast for college and began to dig deeply into theology, discovering the rich history of the Body of Christ. I took classes learning about systematic theology, discovered the riffs in the Church over the years, and came to more deeply appreciate the tenets of the Christian faith and doctrines: His truth that has stood the test of time.

I discovered there are preferences in the Church. The Pauls were telling the Davids to be more theological. The Marys were

live out love

guilting the Marthas to be more relational. My heart broke.

I'm so grateful to have spent a significant amount of time in two different cultures. Hawaii has my heart because that's where I fell in love with Jesus, but the east coast helped me come to understand the depths of that relationship. I have lived on the mainland long enough to begin to look back with nostalgic fondness, treasuring the simple faith of my upbringing—the childlike trust and relational abandonment for a Father who gave His life for us. There is something about the people of Hawaii that is beautiful, pure and child-like in the best possible way. There is an acceptance and trust that comes openly without a need to explain or prove themselves, and I believe that this is the posture that God requires from each of us in order to enter the kingdom. I fear much of Western Christianity has missed the simple truth of the gospel, which says "Unless you change and become like little children, you will never enter the kingdom of heaven" (Matthew 18:3, NIV).

What marks the heart of a child whose innocence has not been lost? Trust. Faith. Hope. Simple love and whole-hearted abandonment. These are all marks of the work of the Holy Spirit, the third and often forgotten member of the Trinity.

Living on the east coast, I have found many churches and believers are too "intellectual" for the Holy Spirit. If it is not something that can be rationally explained or humanly contained, it makes them uncomfortable. Sadly, for the last fifteen years, I've watched the powerlessness of a gospel that speaks His truth but without the supernatural element that declares His authority.

work of the spirit

It's time for the American Church to wake up to their call to holistic surrender to the Creator of the Heavens and the Earth. The two worlds I have been privileged to live in can meet. In fact, they must, in order for us to love the Lord as He has called us to: with our mind, body, soul and spirit. Neither way of worshiping the Lord is better. They both have their place, and they both strengthen the other. While each of us has a preference, I believe we are each called to exercise our faith muscles in all areas.

That has been the focus of my writing and blogging over the past five years: a call to abundant living in the place where God has planted us. We must understand where He has taken us from and where He is sending us, recognizing He has placed each of us in our specific cities and communities for such a time as this! He is asking us to grow our faith muscles and better know Him in ways outside of our comfort zone because it's outside of our security that trust and intimacy is built. That's where faith is fertilized and nourished. As a child trusts His good Father, wholeheartedly and fully surrendered, so we make room for the presence of the Living God to invade our midst.

Stop With the Slogans

When my son was diagnosed with neuroblastoma, the outpouring of love and support was phenomenal. People came out of the woodwork with kind words, notes, meals, you name it. You never feel so loved as when you are walking through a hard place.

live out love

That being said, one of my Hawaiian aunties (whose daughter had also walked through pediatric cancer) warned me I would get the most random and often theologically incorrect statements as attempts to comfort me during that time. I realize now it was just people in their brokenness trying to make sense of areas they had not worked out in their lives. But man, when you are in the trenches of wrestling with God, it stings when people speak things that aren't true.

It made me realize the importance of listening. I don't want to be the person saying things that don't help people in their hardest moments. I don't want to let my brokenness flow onto other people in their times of wrestling and being refined. I don't want to say things that confuse and push them away from the work God is doing in their hearts. I want to be a catalyst for healing and breakthrough!

There is a discernment needed not only in how we communicate, but how we receive. We need to be able to know the true voice of God. I believe this is where the Church is weakest in our day and age. It has become a place to go on Sunday morning to hear His truth. We may even be reading our Bibles and listening to Christian music, but the foundation of the Christian walk is not in doing Christian things, but being in relationship with Him. We are called to hear His voice and understand how He is walking intimately with us in every area of our life. If we aren't seeking to be in relationship with Him, then we will fail to be able to minister to a hurting world around us in a timely and effective way.

work of the spirit

When I met one of my spiritual moms, Ms Rosa, I knew she was the embodiment of a catalyst for healing. As I poured out broken places of my heart and soul to her, she would listen, and before responding, she would often say, "I have some thoughts, but let's see what the Holy Spirit is saying." This is what it looks like to be working by the Spirit. She could have poured her fix into me like many mentors and counselors had done before. She could have told me where I was not loving well, or I was being selfish. Instead, she built a relationship with me.

Call after call, she would listen, pray, validate and offer little nuggets of practical wisdom along the way. It wasn't till about nine months into our relationship that she began to share deeper wisdom and give more direct feedback. I would often ask her to give it to me straight because my heart already felt secure and loved and validated by her. I knew that when she shared what was hard to receive, it came from a place of genuine love and care and desire to see me in freedom.

We are Fighting Spiritual Battles with Human Weapons

Have you ever heard someone speaking out loud of their insecurities and wished you could just show them where to place their trust and security? Have you ever sat with a friend and as they poured out their heart and wished you could hand them all the tools right there that would set them free?

This happens to me often. Probably because I am on a journey to discover my true identity—the amazing freedom I possess and the Hope that I now stand in—and I so desperately want to pull others out of the muck of their own minds. Especially when I see them falling into similar pits I have just jumped out of myself. I want to remind them of the Hope that sets them free. I want to remind them of Whose they are.

But my words are hollow and empty. They are band-aids to their deep heart wounds. We are fighting a spiritual battle with human weapons. The armor of God analogy in Ephesians 6 is one that has been so over taught that often we have lost the power behind it. I don't want to reiterate what so many brilliant teachers have taught on before, but can not brush past this topic without looking afresh at what it is actually saying when it comes to speaking into other's lives.

> For our struggle is not against flesh and blood, but against the rulers, against the authorities, against the powers of this dark world and against the spiritual forces of evil in the heavenly realms. Therefore put on the full armor of God, so that when the day of evil comes, you may be able to stand your ground, and after you have done everything, to stand.
> Ephesians 6: 12-13, NIV

Our enemy is not the person in front of us. We are up against an unseen force that could care less about right and wrong or sound thinking. So when we try to convince our friend or child or spouse with our rational logic, the real enemy laughs. The words may sound right and be theologically accurate to us or people who know us. But if someone is facing spiritual oppression and bondage, my words will clink up against a wall of unbelief and be twisted by the enemy. I have to know what I'm up against. I have to know when to stand, when to love and when to pray. We must learn to use our weapons and armor appropriately. We must learn to fight with weapons of the spirit.

My words may move me, but the Spirit of God alone breathes life into those words that actually seeps into the deep places of human souls and brings healing. It's called the "*rhema*" word of God. It is the active, timely word that He is speaking in specific moments that brings water to a weary soul.

The Rhema Word

"*Rhema*" is defined by Strong's Concordance as an "utterance."[8] It is used at least seventy times in the New Testament. There is much debate in the Church on the theology of this, which is why so many miss out on the power of what God is conveying to us. Most Evangelicals generally believe that any scripture verse is appropriate to use at any time. While the Word of God is "living and active, sharper than any two-edged sword," (Hebrews 4:12, ESV) there is an active tense Word of God being spoken from Heaven by God Himself for every heart need in every specific moment that can actually bring freedom and change to our situations. Sometimes though, we don't get to that place with God because we grow comfortable and satisfied with our here and now. We teach ourselves to accept our "lot," instead of realizing we have a good Daddy who wants to teach us how to activate our faith and cry out to Him so that we might grow and He might show Himself mighty on our behalf.

"Church people" are notorious for throwing around

platitudes and quick fixes to people's pain. It's why there has been a stereotype in film and movies; not just because the enemy is after believers, but also because sometimes the shoe actually fits! If you've ever been a person on the receiving end of these "Christian fixes," you know how annoying it can be. Religion tells us that a scripture verse will heal someone, instead of realizing that it's about being sensitive to the heart issue that an individual is wrestling with so we can speak His truth to the places in which the enemy is lying and see them set free.

The reality is that my encouragement and "advice" can't breathe the Spirit of God into people. I can't find the right word that will speak directly to a wound within, that fills in the holes and satisfies the hunger. I just don't have that kind of power in my strength.

I've seen that power flow through me before, so sometimes the enemy might try to pull a Jesus in the desert trick on me just like He tried to tempt Jesus when He was in a place of weakness. (Luke 4:1-13) He sees my desire to be used, so He tells me I can do it if I take a cheap substitute over the scary, faith free-fall of trusting God. The enemy likes to tell us we can walk in our purpose in a much more convenient way. Instead of having to trust in God's perfect timing, why don't I try to speed it up? Instead of being patient and listening and waiting for the right moment, just share out of turn. Did you know the first time Jesus used the word *"rhema"* was in response to Satan's temptation when he said, "It is written, 'Man shall not live by bread alone, but by every ***rhema*** that proceeds from the mouth

work of the spirit

of God?" (Matthew 4:4, ESV, emphasis and translation added) Jesus chose to push through the feelings of hunger instead of turning the stones into bread. He found His strength and provision in what God had allotted Him. The active Word of God was His food.

The enemy's substitute for the power of God is always more convenient than what God would have us do, but the result is unsatisfying, empty, and without true transformative relief. God's ways are higher and better than our ways. He can be trusted, though the road may seem long.

Friends, we are fighting spiritual battles with man-made tools. We think our words will change a person. We think our theology will prove our point. We think our good works will earn us favor. None of these things are bad things, but when we use them as cheap substitutes for true breakthrough, we will see the emptiness of their power.

I have several friends fighting mental battles in their marriages or health right now. They are questioning why certain close relationships have traits that rub them so raw. They are angry at God for not coming through and rescuing them from the mess and heartbreak. They are waiting on their breakthrough and wondering why they keep revolving around the same mountain and not experiencing the freedom that Christ came to deliver. I would argue that they are all rooted in insecurities from their past. I identify deeply in different shapes and forms. The Lord is rescuing me daily, but my words of compassion and correction fall so flat. My logic ends up convoluted and full of too many points. The Spirit of God alone breathes life. He heals hearts. He renews minds. He convicts souls. He brings the dead back to life.

So why do we even try? Why don't we wait around for God to move? Too often, the part of the Church that recognizes we have nothing to bring to the table has started to preach a false theology of just sitting around and waiting for God to work. They've used "sovereignty" as an excuse to do nothing. That too is the enemy twisting the truth of God.

Here's the crazy part of it all: He wants to use you and me. We are the vessels that He needs to breathe through. For some strange reason, the way He has chosen to set people free is through other people. You and me, we are the instruments He has chosen to work through. We have a part to play.

It's not about people who speak what they want to speak or what seems right to them though. It's not about me saying what I discern and see so that I can "fix" them as quickly as possible. God's ways rarely fit with the "wisdom of this world." As Isaiah 55, reminds us:

> For my thoughts are not your thoughts, neither are your ways my ways," declares the Lord. "As the heavens are higher than the earth, so are my ways higher than your ways and my thoughts than your thoughts."
> Isaiah 55:8-9, NIV

He's looking for surrendered vessels, ready to lay down their seemingly sharp weapons for his supernatural ones. I follow His prompts. I seek Him for wisdom to know when to speak and when

work of the spirit

not to. And when those around me give me feedback that I've been too hard or too soft, I prayerfully seek wise counsel to discern whether what they are saying is or isn't God.

Discerning the Voice of God

One of the most foundational pieces of our Christian walk, that too many Christians are missing out on, is learning how to discern The Voice that matters among the masses of voices coming at us. We have lost the art of silence, stillness, and reflection.

One of my favorite movies of all time is the re-telling of Jesus' birth in, "The Nativity", starring Keisha Castle-Hughes. In an opening scene, one of the teachers in Mary's village is re-telling the Jewish children, in the beautiful oral tradition of the ancient Hebrews, how God spoke to His people throughout history. She reminds them of the word from Elijah (re-written for our modern vernacular):

> "And God said: 'Stand on the sacred mountain'
> And behold, the Lord passed by.
> And a great wind rent the mountain and broke
> in pieces the rocks before the Lord.
> But the Lord was not in the wind.
> And after the wind, an earthquake.
> But the Lord was not in the earthquake.
> And after the earthquake, a fire. But the Lord was not in the fire.
> And after the fire? A still, small voice."9

A still small voice. That is how He always speaks: in the silence, in the stillness, in the quiet. Many of us have not trained our ears to hear our Shepherd's voice. We are so quickly led astray by any wind or philosophy that sounds right; aren't we? Or we are too busy to listen because we have filled our earways with the incessant barrage of information from the news and our social media feeds.

How can we hear His quiet voice in the midst?

One of the most life-changing Bible studies I have ever done is Priscilla Shirer's *Discerning the Voice of God*. Every believer needs to go through this study at least once. Too many of us think we know the Lord's voice, but we don't realize that the enemy's counterfeit has been camouflaged to look so similar to the Shepherd's that only one who is currently spending extensive time with Him would know the difference.

How do you know, when you have two different "good" options, which one He's in? How do you learn to discern the voice of God? By spending time with Him, knowing His heart, His character. His way always satisfies in the long term, but often, in the short term, it is hard or not as attractive.

Too many of us think we can choose whatever path we would like, and He will bless it just because that's what He does. But who is running the show in that picture? It's not the King of Kings, but rather the creation. Isaiah says: "Your ears will hear a voice behind you, saying, 'This is the way; walk in it'" (Isaiah 30:21, NIV). Our knowledge will not always lead us in the right way, but quietly leaning on the one who holds eternity in His hands will lead to life and peace.

In 2018, I participated in a cohort called "Unveiled" (started by the former prayer director of the International Justice

work of the spirit

Mission). The goal of our time together was to fine tune our voices as we listened to His, and it was one of the most transformative experiences of my life. Most of us went in because we knew there was a call on our life. What we didn't realize was that our call was finding His voice. As we learned to sit with Him, we learned to hear what He was speaking. From that place we could actually use our voices for what they were created. We all had lots of passions and ideas going in, but we came out realizing the power of waiting to speak when He tells us to.

God has a specific word for His people for every single moment. It is our joy and our call to learn to listen for His voice to direct us to speak to their pain. But will we? It is only those listening who will be able to access power and actually watch lives set free.

The *rhema* word of God outweighs religious jargon every time!

∞

Let's stop fighting with the wrong tools, Church. Our good theology and our well-meaning compassion, they are nice, but they aren't life changing. Transformative change comes through surrendered vessels willing to admit their own lack of strength. It's when surrendered individuals stand up with courage and the fragrance of humility that the Spirit of God breathes through them to the deep wounds in others.

It's His love shining through and His well-timed words

that speak to the wounds. His Spirit at work in us is power, and I want to walk in that power; the power that resurrected Christ from the dead that dwells in you and me. "And if the Spirit of him who raised Jesus from the dead is living in you, he who raised Christ from the dead will also give life to your mortal bodies because of his Spirit who lives in you" (Romans 8:11, NIV).

Here is the good news: We can walk in that power, if we surrender! When we choose to stop looking at others' differences and instead, through grace, see the diverse beauty of the Body of Christ, everything changes. We begin to fight for unity, as we humbly confess that He is working through different people in ways we don't always understand. When the Holy Spirit helps us lay down our plans and preferences, and we acknowledge that He is the Author (not us) tying all of the stories of the Bride together, we begin to walk in freedom. As we continue to allow Him to do the work in us, it creates a space for Him to set the world free through our humble trust and surrender. He is indeed bringing freedom to the world, and He's using His church in all of her multiple facets and flavors. We, however, can only be a part of it if we lay down ours and pick up His tools instead.

Let's not waste another moment trying to impart the power of God and transformative change without the Spirit of God. We as a Church must begin everything we do with prayer — stillness and listening for the voice of our Father. Our service, new ministries, new projects, new books, starting a family,

work of the spirit

fighting through old habits—everything we do must be covered in prayer. That is the secret ingredient that opens our eyes to a spiritual realm and the tools at our disposal that will bring down giants in our midst.

Get out of THE WAY

> Set a guard, O Lord, over my mouth;
> keep watch over the door of my lips!
> Psalm 141:3, ESV

Did you know we can be the very ingredient that blocks our own break-through? God is a gentleman, and He doesn't force us to obey. His will will always be fulfilled in our lives, but the abundance that should come through that process is only reaped through obedience to His call. The most famous Biblical example is the Israelites in the desert. It was supposed to take one year to enter Canaan, but instead they spent forty years traveling in circles. Talk about frustrating! I've seen it happen many times in my life too; even over the course of getting this book to release.

Oh that we would become a people who live hourly on our knees—that we would live lives marked by the flavor of Jesus—that we would wait for Him to lead, rather than us trying to lead Him.

I mentioned in chapter 2, that I had individuals in my life who sought to help "fix" me. Many of them spoke the truth that God later used in my life. At the time, I felt force-fed on a time frame that they were trying to impose. Instead of waiting for my heart to be ready, they pushed scripture on me that they wanted me to hear at that moment. Instead of working with God for my healing, they added extra boulders for me to have to push through.

How often have I done the exact same thing? How often have I seen a gaping character flaw in my husband or my kids and tried to fix the situation immediately? If they would just listen to me, we could avoid all the things I think they should avoid and live happily ever after.

God's plans are so different from ours. He chose the foolish to shame the wise. He chooses situations and circumstances we would not choose to do the perfect work of refinement and character shaping we so desperately need.

Sometimes the one person who is in the way of a breakthrough is me. Too often it's God's own people who get in His way of doing something that would overwhelm and astound.

My friend, Nikki, recently shared a story of how God transformed her life in middle school. Her mom, who had recently been saved, wanted to help bring some Biblical perspective to her daughter's dating life, but when she saw how hostilely Nikki responded to her prompts, she immediately backed off. She said she knew the Holy Spirit was already at work. Within the year, Nikki had a truly transformative come-to-Jesus that changed her desires to the things of God. Imagine how long that process would have taken if her mom had continued to push and prod and cajole?

If only we could learn from my friend's mom. When people start responding to our feedback in defense, most likely we've hit a nerve. At that point, it's time to let the Holy Spirit do His thing.

Our job is not to create programs to fix people's needs. Our job is to create space for the Spirit of the living God to do His work. Our job is to get ourselves out of the way and function as vessels that He can move in and through.

Leaders are Listeners

What do you think of when you hear the word leader? Someone standing in a pulpit delivering a message? Perhaps you think of your boss or some business executive who is the one calling the shots. Our culture has misunderstood true leadership. We think it's the person with the title–the one doing all the talking. We think leaders are the ones who get to tell others what to do.

Jesus was the exact opposite. He changed the world on his knees. He changed the world while washing feet.

The best Bible studies I have ever been in were not "taught." Instead, the leaders created space for others to learn and hear from God for themselves. They helped bring order to the group. They often helped re-direct conversations that were getting off topic. Their goal was not to pour out their wisdom, but to help others discover His.

This is one thing I loved in the training model for Community Bible Study (CBS), an internationally recognized and beloved Bible study program used all over the world. I served with a TCBS ministry in northern Virginia, for over six years in my early twenties, and I really appreciated the training program we were required to go through to lead. Some of the most fruitful learning and growth for me happened in those groups. The CBS trainer's manual reminds those in positions of leadership that our role is not to be a fountain of truth that everyone comes to listen to, but instead a facilitator who creates space for the true Fountain to flow.

While His truth is always the same, it flavors itself uniquely for each heart. We come from different family backgrounds and different deeply ingrained perspectives and convictions. God is big enough to understand it all. He made it all. Walking with Him is not limited to one particular denomination or cultural preference.

I have, unfortunately, had leaders who loved to do all the talking. They loved to push their perspective of the world on others. Instead of having ears to listen and hearts humble to realize they are but a piece of the puzzle, they often verbalized that if I would just listen to them, they would be able to help me figure out my problems. I wanted to believe them. I tried many times to reinvent my life to fit the model they prescribed.

get out of the way

No human being will ever be capable of fixing another. We are all signposts pointing to the Great Healer. What we have to offer is limited and will run out. What He offers is a well that will never run dry. Our job is to lead others to the bottomless river of Jesus Himself. He is, by far, the best counselor I have ever had. He is firm but kind. He is the best listener. He alone gets me and speaks to the deep places in my heart. Only He knows every facet of me. He designed me in my mom's womb with a plan and a purpose. He alone knows how to unlock the heart and heal the broken parts that my sin and this broken world have destroyed.

Our churches and our homes are crying out for leaders to step up and live by example, listening first and foremost to the heart of God and secondly to the needs of those they serve; living not for the applause of others but for an Audience of One.

I mentioned my father in the introduction of this book because he modeled this so well for me. I asked him one time how he became a listener. He told me that it wasn't because he was good at it or had a propensity towards it. He found himself in a home full of talkers and people wanting to be heard (I being the paramount offender), and he realized it was something he could do. So he trained himself to not only hear words, but to try and understand hearts.

Growing up, he knew my heart in a unique way and sought to fully understand it like few friends ever have. As a young girl looking for truth, that attracted me to the Father of all fathers' heart. My dad's example pointed to someone far greater and bigger than him. There was something in him that kept funneling me back to the one who could truly hear and meet the needs of my heart. He saw me when my heart needed a safe place, and that is the same thing Jesus did for us. He saw us as we were and called us still. He doesn't see our mistakes; He sees His image imprinted on us, His beloved ones. When we are able to see others the way He sees us, then we will truly love.

Wasted Anointing: The Character Principle

Saul, the first King of Israel, has always fascinated me in a heartbreaking way. Here was a man chosen and anointed by Yahweh's prophet to lead God's people. He started off with such promise, yet he ended his life at war with God, trying to suppress the move of God (aka David) in the next generation. Of his own volition, and understanding what he was doing, he decided to try to kill off the very work God was doing (see the killing of an entire family of priests in 1 Samuel 22). How did Saul get to this place?

In case you want to argue that Saul was actually never used by God, take another look at his story. In 1 Samuel 10:10, and 11:6, we see that it was the Spirit of God that rushed upon Saul and worked through him. This man was not only chosen by God and anointed by His prophet, but he was used specifically to speak to Israel through prophecy on two documented occasions.

get out of the way

God used this man. However, the truth of the matter is that every time Saul was crossed or called to account, the true colors of his heart were revealed, and they always worshiped at the altar of his own image.

In 1 Samuel 13, after Saul successfully fights off the Philistines, he unlawfully sacrifices burnt offerings instead of waiting for the priest to do it. It says in verse eight, that he even waited the proper number of days, but when he saw that the people were scattering, he rushed into handling the situation himself.

I can identify with Saul here. I have often rushed into doing the "Christian thing" instead of waiting for God's timing. I have tried to push God's hand to act because I want to get things done. Saul is all about image and meeting goals, and he misses out on God doing it for him because he tries to force it by his own might. Sometimes we get in the way of God doing amazing things because of our willfulness.

Samuel, the Prophet, confronted Saul. Here was a chance for this gifted man to make things right and get back on track. Here was a chance for repentance and owning up to his own need for God, so the Spirit of God could continue to use him. Here was a chance for the character developed in conviction to take root. Instead, Saul rejected making it right with the Lord. His eyes were on his own kingdom and not on the heart of God. This is the clincher to why Saul missed out on his kingdom being established forever: he put the blessing ahead of the one who gave it to Him. He got in his own way.

There is a word here for anyone who has ears to hear.

How many of us have lost sight of relationship with God because we were in pursuit of happiness, a husband, a family, a good marriage, a vibrant ministry…? How many of us can so easily replace the Giver with the gift? How easily can we find ourselves, like Saul, getting in the way of God's miraculous power because we think we need to hold onto it with our own hands? If we are not able to grapple daily with our need for God, He can never use us in the places that need transformation in our lives.

So Samuel prophesies that Saul will be replaced by "a man after God's own heart;" a man who is ready to repent and lay aside his plans for God's better ones.

Second Chances

Don't forget; God is gracious beyond what we can understand or comprehend. He's the God of second chances. He's the God of redemption. Saul's story does not have to end here. God gives him many chances.

In 1 Samuel 15, Saul decides to count his army. Saul is motivated by numbers and influence, and worse yet, he sets up a monument to himself in verse 12. What modern day monuments do we set up for ourselves? Do social media accounts come to mind? What about ministries dedicated to our name and fame? Many people get so caught up in their role as a mother or a position in a company or among their peers that they forget their first allegiance. The most devious of misalignments are the ones wrapped in "good things."

get out of the way

When the heart is correctly engaged, there is no issue, but when the heart is holding on to something for one's own name and fame, the facade often makes it hard to discern it as a foe. For example: family and ministry are both important and honorable goals to attend to. However, they can quickly become idols, if we find our identity and worth in them. At first the misplaced allegiance may seem unnoticeable or hardly worth the time to address. But little by little, misaligned worship always becomes a full blown issue. You don't notice it until someone attempts to call out your blind spot. If you respond with defensiveness and hostility, then you know that this good thing has become your very own golden calf.

Samuel calls out Saul for not completely destroying the Amalekites as he was called to. Instead, Saul held onto the spoils. Here is Saul's chance at redemption. Make it right. Don't waste your anointing! Instead, he compounds the heartbreak. As he is being reprimanded by the prophet of the Lord, Saul responds, "I have obeyed the voice of the Lord" (1 Samuel 15:20, ESV). He justifies himself, even arguing that the sheep and goats are to be dedicated to the Lord in sacrifice. Saul refused to give this second chance an opportunity to free his soul. He chose to hold on to what he thought he needed most, and he did it wrapped in a "religious facade" of "obeying the law." How many of us have tried that one? "It's for God, so I can justify my sin." The conviction that would bring freedom to his soul evaporates. Saul built a taller wall. He further entrenched himself as his own god and went to war with the one who put him in that position.

What a waste of an anointing! What a sad end to the story of a man who held such promise. Saul was the one who got in the way of God using him for dynamic things. He had all the equipment and even the favor of the Lord, but he wasted it. He wanted it the way he wanted it. He didn't want to wait for God's way and time. The thing he most wanted could have been his, but God wanted his heart first, and Saul would rather have held onto his earthly kingdom and treasures than his relationship with the Lord. He had his priorities all wrong. If we don't learn a lesson from Saul, and continue to hold on to our shortcomings, when they are repeatedly brought to our attention, we won't become the effective agents of change He designed us to be. This is not a call to be perfect. Instead, when we allow our weakness to bring us to our knees, His strength can then be manifested in our lives.

How many of us think that our religious rituals and spirit-led work is somehow what God wants? He wants our hearts, not our sacrifice. As Samuel reminds Saul:

> "Has the Lord as great delight in burnt offerings and sacrifices, as in obeying the voice of the Lord? Behold, to obey is better than sacrifice, and to listen than the fat of rams."
> 1 Samuel 15:22, ESV

How often does this spirit of self-righteousness and lack of self-awareness cause us to miss out on the opportunity to be set free from our shortcomings? How often have we, like Saul, put "things of God" first so that we can appear godly to the people who matter? We pour ourselves into motherhood or ministry for

get out of the way

the sake of doing the godly thing but completely miss the mark on our first calling, which is our relationship with God.

God is after our hearts. He is after a relationship with us. All the other stuff we do is rubbish if it isn't rooted in obedience to Him.

This story is not just shared so we can judge Saul. It's the story of where each of us is headed if we don't acknowledge the beast called sin living in each of us. So how do we respond to this charge? How do we lay down our image of perfection? Can we step into freedom by dismantling the desire and action to control our own lives?

I know the answer for each of us boils down to repentance. If we can identify and confess the areas in our life where we have sinned, "times of refreshing may come from the Lord" (Acts 3:19-20, NIV). When conviction comes, our job is to acknowledge our sin and to ask for the Lord to cleanse us. If we know we struggle with fearing man over God, we need to confess it. If we have chosen a way that seems right to us over what God has asked us to do, we need to repent.

Is anything bubbling to the surface of your heart right now? Don't downplay it. Don't push it to the side. I can guarantee that the Spirit of God is working, even now, to bring to your attention that from which He longs to set you free.

The problem is, we think we still need these cages. We are okay with living in the chains of our bondage, judgment and idolatry. We think the conviction we are feeling is actually someone else's fault rather than embracing their words of truth that could free our souls. As C.S. Lewis famously wrote, "God whispers to us in our pleasures, speaks in our conscience, but shouts in our pain: it is His megaphone to rouse a deaf world."[10] Instead of viewing pain as a wake up call, we run away from it. We run to the justification and defensiveness that feel good but are actually tools of the enemy that entrap us from truly living. Instead of letting God remove the areas in us that don't reflect Him, we hold on to these broken areas in our lives and call it "safety." We like it when we know what to expect. We like our cages of bitterness, unforgiveness and accusation. We like being self-sufficient, secure and in charge of our lives.

We need to start cultivating His perspective. We are living in cages of our own making. We are getting in the way of God's moving, and if we could hear the Samuels in our lives who speak out of love and a true desire to see us set free, we could actually see the power of God at work in our lives.

Will you join me today in surrendering those areas that He is bringing to the surface? Your Father in Heaven who loves you so much wants to see you set free today! You are holding the keys to the freedom He has already purchased for you. Will you utilize what is already at your disposal?

get out of the way

◦— Say this prayer with me —◦

Jesus, we confess to You our desire to have applause of man over serving and obeying You. We repent of our need to be better than others and have our way. We ask You to forgive us for complaining about the story you have chosen to write for our lives. We want to be vessels fully cleaned out so that You might pour Your new wine in us and use us as You see fit. We were created to glorify You. We were designed to testify of You and You alone. Help us in our weakness and our sin. We aim to honor. We want every second to point to You. Help us to be men and women after Your heart and Your heart alone. Everything else will fade away, but You Jesus, You are forever!

7

Good does not EQUAL GOD

> But he said to me, 'My grace is sufficient for you, for my power is made perfect in weakness.' Therefore I will boast all the more gladly of my weaknesses, so that the power of Christ may rest upon me. For the sake of Christ, then, I am content with weaknesses, insults, hardships, persecutions, and calamities. For when I am weak, then I am strong.
> 2 Corinthians 12:9-10, NIV

I have a confession to make. I've known about Jesus my entire life, but I have only come to understand what it means to let Him be Lord of my life about seven years ago.

This may come as a surprise to those who know me. You see, I've led Bible studies for more than a decade, ministered to teens, prayed for friends, checked in with those struggling, and done countless service opportunities. My life was a poster child for "good Christian kid." Yet, I still lived in bondage to my sin and pride. Touches with the Holy Spirit lasted only a short time because somehow I thought I had earned the right to be with Him because I managed to not drink and sleep around in college. Silly me. It wasn't until 2017, that I fully understood the gospel freed me from my need to always be doing stuff for God. You see, I knew the truth, but the truth had not yet set me free.

Do not misunderstand what I am saying. I'm not giving us a pass to keep our faith to ourselves and never speak into others' lives. This confession is not making an excuse for us to sit around and let our "faith be personal." If we love Jesus, it should show and flow out of every fiber of our being. We won't be able to shut up about Him because who He is will reach every part of our mind, body, soul and spirit. The world will have to stop and realize that our lives have been changed.

However, you see; I had the opposite problem. Much of the works of my life didn't flow from a heart overflowing with gratefulness to a good God. There was a lot of "religious busyness." There were lots of church events and meetings and sweet moments with people who spend time with Him. Yet while I tasted His presence and experienced Him, He wasn't perpetually Lord of my life—the one calling the shots. I was still in the driver's seat, and I would occasionally turn the wheel over to Him. You know, just in those moments when I really needed Him.

It takes the grace of God to reveal this seemingly "non-issue." You see; I saw His hands in so many little details. I have experienced the Holy Spirit at work in my heart my entire life. I have tasted deep and intimate moments with the Lord of the universe since I was six years old. Real stuff. Still, much of my life has been unknowingly works-based.

My mom had a chart for us to mark off when we read our

good does not equal God

Bible and did our chores. While I'm so grateful the Word of God was taught in my home and that my mind is familiar with His truths, much of the motion of reading through my Bible was to get that check and not to actually sit and meet with God. Going to a conservative Christian college only further emphasized this desire to get high marks for doing the "good stuff." I think being in these protected environments ended up having a negative impact on my heart. Perhaps you can identify? Instead of tasting His freedom, I became further chained to a desire to get approval with the "right people."

One of my dearest friends recently challenged me: "Do you just want the fruit that God has to give, or do you actually want to meet with God?" This was such a hard question to answer because it spoke to the idol in my heart into which I had turned God's good and perfect gifts. I had turned intimacy with Him into a brownie badge that I could pin on my puffed up chest. I wanted God, but I wanted the fruit too. If there wasn't any fruit, would we still want God? That's the harder question.

I've been on a journey of discovering that surrender is where the sweetest fruit is. He is the best thing this life has to offer. Walking in obedience to Him, even when the circumstances don't change, is what this relationship is all about. That's where my heart is changed, and I realize He is all my heart desires. He doesn't need me to do anything. Instead, I get to do missions with Him. I get to be used by Him to be a chain breaker. There is such a narrow difference between simply doing good and good pouring out of a heart surrendered to God. The flavor and texture of the fruit is night and day—like the differences between generic and organic eggs. If you don't know what I'm talking about, you need to try some real eggs. Real food will change your life—and your taste buds. But I digress.

Doing good in our own strength is distasteful. That doesn't mean that sometimes we won't have to say things that are hard or that people don't like. His truth is offensive to those who love their flesh. But when we continue to speak truth in love, the fruit of our heart is revealed even when we have to say hard things.

What I am speaking to is the attempt to be godly without obedience; the speaking of truth without ever doing the hard work of love. This type of Christianity is powerless. But obeying His voice and loving when it goes against our flesh, that creates an environment for healing. Surrender and humility paired with His truth breaks strongholds.

The Gospel is Not a Formula

I share because I have met so many well-meaning moms and dads and walked with so many offspring of such well-meaning parents who thought that certain circles, influences, or ways of raising their kids was the same as running after Christ. I have watched the confusion and chains that continue to hold these beautiful souls down. They thought they had fully found Jesus. They sang of freedom on Sundays, but like

good does not equal God

me, they hadn't actually fully tasted it yet. Satan had watered down God's life-giving water with an unsatisfying substitute, and in the Church no less.

So many "good things" can appear to be God's way, but that's how the enemy works. He gets as close to the real thing as He can to distract us from the life-giving source. Jesus' ways do not look like this world's. They don't fit a certain formula. The seemingly right way of doing things (or God's call for someone else) is not the same thing as the fresh "manna" and sustenance He has for you. You can try to go by the book—try to turn your Christian walk or parenting into a formula. But once you have experienced authentic Christian living, you can smell and taste the difference. Nothing else will do.

Don't be distracted by the bells and whistles of something that seems "fool-proof." That has all the markings of a deceiver who likes to twist good things. If you think there is anything outside of Jesus to save your kids (homeschool, Awana, only Christian shows), it's time to re-think your theology. It's Jesus + nothing. Don't listen to the lies of the enemy that say you need to be a different person or pile rules and expectations on your kids in order to have them act right.

Don't believe the untruths that say YOU need to make sure your kids know Jesus and say the sinner's prayer or they will never make it. They are His, and He has never messed up or missed an opportunity to draw all men to Himself. Your job is simply to live as an instrument that displays Christ at work in you. You get to be a picture of Jesus to them and trust that He will call them to Him in His perfect time and way. Your honesty and humility will speak loudly. Your honesty about your need for Christ is where the power is. They see you working out your faith, and that means more than any facade of perfection that they can see through anyway. And guess what; letting go of the lie that you need to "save your kids" and provide the "perfect environment" will set you free! You can be a catalyst for healing in your family by simply being authentic about your need for Jesus.

Run to the Rock that is higher. Let's learn to hear His voice so we can tell a counterfeit from the real deal. Doing good only gets you so far and leaves you feeling empty. It's the Holy Spirit alive in you that opens your spouse, kid, neighbor, and colleague's eyes to a bigger reality. Run to Truth. Run to Freedom. Don't be subject to the yoke of slavery of appearance, going with Christian culture or doing what everyone else is doing. Let's let our kids, our marriages, and our communities dance in the freedom that Jesus came for. He alone saves, and He uses broken and imperfect people.

His Strength is Magnified in Our Weakness

It seems that every Christian on their journey to becoming more like Christ struggles with the idea of perfectionism. We want to be like Christ, and sometimes we put ourselves there before our character has had a chance to be perfected to be more like Him. We want to be the one to find a shortcut to holiness, so we look for ways to speed up the sanctification process.

good does not equal God

Maybe it is because we were all made for Eden and perfection, so we are hard on ourselves, wanting to be all that we were originally created to be. I have a standard of excellence in my mind, and when I don't meet it, I can be extremely disappointed in myself. I find that most Christians hold themselves and others up to an impossible standard of perfection.

The deep truth I have discovered in my journey is this: when I am weak, then I find my absolute place of strength (2 Corinthians 12:10, NIV). For it's only when I'm weak that I realize my need for someone stronger to help me. It's in letting go of my versions of safety and control that I find true transformation. It's when I can actually let go of the escape patterns in my life and my attempts at reforming myself, and instead look to the one who desires to see me set free and has already prepared the way, that I realize my worth and the freedom that has already been purchased for me.

It's when I'm weak, I realize His strength is mine. All I have to do is give up control of doing it my way and let Him do His thing. He draws us out right at our breaking point and shows us the expanse of freedom that is ours, our birthright as children of the Most High God.

How do you find those places where you still need to be set free? I have discovered a couple ways to identify the areas He is bringing to the surface.

Identifying Perspective Wake Up Calls

Have you ever noticed that the people who rub you the

live out love

wrong way all tend to have a common link? They all seem to rub you the wrong way in the same way. I have mulled over this for years. How come the people who irk me most usually do it the same way, even if they are from completely different cultures and backgrounds and time periods in my life? Over the years, God has seen fit to bring the same type of person into my life, over and over and over. You'd think He was sending me a signal! My dad always told me He was, but I didn't quite know what he meant. It was irksome, and I would rather he had hugged me and said, "Yes; that person is annoying, and you do deserve better friends."

One Sunday, my husband and I were sitting in a marriage discussion group at church sharing our stories, and two people at the table started irking me in "that" way. The issue: their pride. This one particular issue seems to raise its head a lot. Does nobody else notice this? I wondered. Everyone seemed to be nodding in agreement, fascinated by their story. I even asked my husband if he noticed it—Nope. He tends to, though, notice something different in others repeatedly.

This is how it all clicked for me. My husband notices flaws in others that I see in him. He points out things in me and others that sometimes seem to come out of left-field, and I want to say, "Hey! That's your issue!" Then the mirror got turned on me. The issue I see in others, that's my issue! The pride and arrogance I see in others, that is my issue. That is my sin. These people are simply helping carve out the sin in my heart. The defensiveness rising in my spirit is a

good does not equal God

sign of the issue God is asking me to give to Him that He might make me into His image. The book of Matthew reminds us, "For in the same way you judge others, you will be judged, and with the measure you use, it will be measured to you" (Matthew 7:2, NIV).

I never saw that verse so clearly as I do now. The way I judge, I will be judged. I am measured by this same measure. Luke poignantly wrote in chapter 6, "Out of the overflow of the mouth, the heart speaks" (Luke 6:45, BSB). My heart's true measuring stick is revealed in my opinions of others, particularly those who annoy me.

When the Holy Spirit revealed this to me for the umpteenth time, it spoke straight to the self-serving worship I am so prone to fall into. My sin. My judgmental heart. My desperate need for a Savior.

Too many Christians are convicted of their sin but don't take the next step of walking in the freedom that Christ died to give. We walk around with a world watching, not wanting any part of the brokenness. Christians aware of their sin, but not walking in the cure. This should not be. God doesn't leave us in this place, friends. No.

We are called to walk in victory. Christ came to set us free, to relieve us of "the chains of slavery" (Galatians 5:1, NIRV). What does that look like? How do we walk in freedom once we become aware of our sin?

My tendency or fleshly cop-out in the past has been to "pray for" those people at the table with issues. "Wow, they are struggling with pride. I will pray God makes that clear to them so their poor spouse doesn't have to suffer."

How often we all fall into this trap. You know why? Editing others fixes the conviction starting to play out in our soul. We don't have to look at our sin issue because we are praying for our friend's issue. Read that one more time because this is the difference between life and death in your relationships! We cover up our inability to change by shifting the blame to others.

Defensiveness traps us in our sin. Is this not what Christians in America are often blamed for? We are told that we come across as Pharisees, and perhaps we are blamed for that because that's exactly what we do when we don't let His light of conviction change us. If we can't deal with our issues first, we can not offer anything to the world. You can only authentically share what you have been truly transformed by. Otherwise, we are like dishonest car salesmen, trying to share something that we don't have the ability to prove works. Someone searching can see right through that. They are looking for the real deal. They need something that transforms and changes their reality.

The issue is not finding our sin, but realizing the kindness of a Savior to save us from ourselves—to realize we are broken and messed up. Christ came while we were still broken to set us free. His love is unconditional – never gives up, never turns its back.

I used to think the parable of the prodigal son in Luke 15 was unfair. No matter how far we run, God will take us back. Isn't this a formula to encourage people to take advantage of grace and do whatever they want? In the short-term, perhaps it may seem like that, but God is not a God with short-term plans. He has a long-term plan. A love like His is convicting as

good does not equal God

it draws us back. Who would want to fail a love that never gives up, no matter how mocked or scorned? That is love we all dream of having but never truly experience in another human. There is one person who can love like that, and He came for you and me and hung on a tree to prove His love.

Next time someone rubs you the wrong way, realize that is the Lord drawing you to Himself. He is trying to give you a picture of your heart, so you might come running back to him. Like the prodigal son, we each have taken our share of His blessings and run away. We are not complete without the love of a Father who will never give up on us, no matter how black our heart. When we walk in that freedom, it's amazing how it wipes away our judgmental nature.

I went back to that table discussion the following week, and people's brokenness did not rub me the wrong way because the spotlight was no longer on the sin rising in me but on a Savior who so graciously forgave me of all my filth. My confession and accepting His sacrifice for my wrongs set me free to forgive and intercede for others instead of judging their blindness.

2 Corinthians 12:9-10 should be a lifestyle declaration for anyone who calls themselves a follower of Christ:

> But he said to me, "My grace is sufficient for you, for my power is made perfect in weakness." Therefore I will boast all the more gladly about my weaknesses, so that Christ's power may rest on me. That is why, for Christ's sake, I delight in weaknesses, in insults, in hardships, in persecutions, in difficulties. For when I am weak, then I am strong.
> 2 Corinthians 12:9-10, NIV

Live out Love

It's in our place of brokenness that victory is won, and we have the opportunity to give credit to whom credit is truly due. The place of my deepest mess-ups is the place of His greatest transformation! Where I am weak, where I don't have it all together, where I feel like I'm losing my mind, that is my place of freedom. It is not in bragging about my weakness but instead boasting in the power of the cross that rescues me from a place of bondage.

I'll talk more in chapter 9, "The Power of Repentance," about what to do with the places of conviction that He is bringing to the surface, and the importance of humility in being a catalyst for healing in our families and communities. But before we do that, I want to take you a little deeper into my story. God took this issue of my weakness being my strength and cracked open a whole area of bondage in my heart that was so closely tied to my "faith" that I wouldn't have known it was an issue if He hadn't made it a focus again and again and again. When you ask God to make you more like Him, He always delivers! He really wants us to find our strength in Him alone.

∽

Are you ready to see transformation and breakthrough in your life and the lives around you? Christ is ready for His bride to rise up. He needs us to fight the spiritual fight with Him, but the weapons He needs us to use are born out of humility and dying to ourselves. They are born out of our weaknesses and our insecurities. They are born from the darkest and hardest places of

good does not equal God

our lives—that's where He wants to come through and use us to break down tall towers of darkness. His Spirit breathing through the redeemed brokenness of our lives that He has healed has the power to demolish spiritual strongholds in heavenly realms. Jesus alone can break through layers of false thinking, deep hurts, and family history, and bring healing oil that cleanses every part of the people we so long to see set free.

He works through our surrender and trust, not our striving. It's okay that we are weak, because our weakness invites His strength. So are we ready to get out of the driver's seat and let Him be God in our lives?

I encourage you to embrace your weakness and find others who do too. Not just the tidied up versions of "perfect Christians" that are trying to have it all together, but the deeply broken, *I need Jesus* places. For when you are weak, then *He is strong!*

There's something about His power displayed in our weakness. It's when we figure out we bring nothing to the table that He can finally step in and use us as instruments in the Perfect Designer's hands.

But it takes us getting our eyes off of trying to have it all together and instead looking to the one who does. That's when the Spirit of God can break through and do the impossible; not by might, not by power, but by His Spirit.

In the next chapter you will see how He did just that in my life. So buckle up, it's about to get a little bumpy.

8

Making new
WINESKINS

> Neither do people pour new wine into old wineskins.
> If they do, the skins will burst; the wine will run out and the
> wineskins will be ruined. No, they pour new wine into new
> wineskins, and both are preserved.
> Matthew 9:17, NIV

Have you ever had a really good glass of wine? You know; the $100 stuff, where you can taste the full body of the grape? There is a special process required to get the very best glass of wine. A good bottle doesn't happen by simply picking a grape off a vine. There is a development process for the fruit. The longer it stays on the vine, the more complex the flavor is. The more developed and softened tannins that provide a smoother flavor, result from grapes that have been harvested after several seasons of vine growth. Patience and skill are required of the winemaker. The vine must be ready.

Then there is the crushing process. It takes meticulous friction and pressure to gently squeeze the juice from the grape. Too much of the skin would make the wine too bitter

live out love

to enjoy. It takes skill and more patience to do it right.

Those are just the early steps before the fermentation process. There are many more years of waiting before that bottle ever gets to your table, so when we hand over an hour's worth of wages for a good bottle of wine, we are honoring a process that may have taken ten to fifteen years.

So it is with our lives. If we want to live a life full of fruit that flavors conversations and changes the communities we walk into, it is going to require a special refining process. The best wine from you and me requires the massaging and pressure of a master's hands; one who knows how to skillfully get the best flavor that will bless the world we live in.

I don't know about you, but I'm tired of what little ol' me brings to the table. I don't want to serve the world "Christianese" and Bible verses without the power of the Spirit behind those words. I want to walk in the mantle and anointing of the Holy Spirit of God, and that requires surrendering.

Those of us raised in the Church often forget that our pat encouragements to people in pain (like "God's sovereign" or "The joy of the Lord is our strength" to someone battling discouragement) doesn't heal the ache in human hearts. Yes, God is sovereign, and He will be glorified no matter what, but He is a gentleman. He does not force His way on us. Instead, He woos us. He pursues us with relentless love because He wants us to experience Him in His fullness. It's called free will, and it's what makes this tangible love relationship so desirable—being wanted and changed from the inside out. If we would let Him do it, we would be astounded at what He wants to do in our midst. Hillsong's song "*New Wine*" reminds me that in the crushing, He is making a new wine.

Sometimes we think life is all about our vision that fits into our perspective of His kingdom. But the ways of God are opposite the ways of man. It's in the surrender of what we think we need and what we think He represents that He gives us the most satisfying thing of all: the presence of the Living God. If you want to experience more than what you are seeing and witness the power of God at work in your life, then you are going to have to let Him have His way. And there are probably areas in your life you equate with following Him that may need deeper refining and surrender.

I love how worship teams like Maverick City Music, Elevation Worship, and many others are not content to stay stagnant singing old songs but instead have taken the Psalmist seriously in Psalm 33:3, to "sing a new song." "*New Wine*" became my anthem of freedom in 2019, as the next wave of this life adventure with God rushed into my peripheral vision. This is because the hard parts of our life don't happen so others can pity us. We aren't victims of our circumstances. Yes; there is warfare. Yes; there is a spiritual attack, but I have a good Father working in and through all things for my good, as I surrender to His process, and "no weapon formed against me shall prosper" (Isaiah 54:17, NIV) when I am sheltered under the refuge of His wings (Psalm 91: 4, NIV).

Behold, He is doing something new (Isaiah 43:19, NIV), but it requires stepping back on the altar and surrendering to a loving master's touch.

Making the Wineskins

I think all of us desire to see a move of God in our midst; a touch from Heaven that restores broken relationships and heals diseases, but I think a lot of us miss out on enjoying and reaping the fruit of God moving because we aren't willing to surrender the areas of our life that He needs to refine in the fire. Hard circumstances in our life are not guaranteed to be character-shaping experiences. We must allow the potter to do His thing or we will find ourselves in similar circumstances over and over in our lives. It's God's way of lovingly trying to help us become more like Him.

In Matthew 9, Jesus explains that new wine can not be poured into old wineskins or the skins will burst, and the wine will run out. Instead, new wine is poured into new wineskins so that both are preserved. When a wineskin becomes old, it no longer holds the liquid well. The goat skin becomes brittle and full of cracks. If new wine (with new fermentation) is poured inside, it will create a crack in the old skin and leak out.

I've been spending a lot of time studying wineskins (in light of the passage on new wine in Matthew 9) and the need for us to be flexible to how God is currently moving. A wineskin was the container used in ancient times for the transportation of wine, milk, oil, and water. It was made from the whole hide of a goat that

making new wineskins

had been carefully cut, heated, dried and then massaged with oil. This laborious process produced an airtight, waterproof container that would allow its owner to transport essential refreshment over miles of hot desert. Once emptied, it became brittle and cracked, which would allow any new liquid poured into it to seep out. Thus the need to make "new wineskins." In order to become functional again, the deceased goat's hide needed to be massaged and oiled to regain its elasticity and functionality.

No wonder Jesus referred to this analogy so often. It is a perfect picture of what sanctification in the believer's life looks like. He pours His spirit into us, but over time we get comfortable or callous or lazy, and we have to go back to the refiner's fire to be made fresh and new for Him to work in and through us. If we are unable to bend a knee and shift with what God is doing, the people under us will suffer. They will experience our brokenness instead of a refreshing sip of His presence. We don't want people to see us and our preferences based on personal experience. If we speak from a place of the flesh, with ill-timed words, that's all they will hear: our gripe.

We were made for more. We were made to be Kingdom builders in others' hearts. We want them to see Him. That can only happen when we live whole in Him and surrender to His timing and an understanding of their hearts. If we choose to give only our take on something, without the love for their backgrounds, they will most likely be tripped up by our personal pet theological nuances. They will experience our twisted theology as we try to protect our blind spots rather than the pure truth. We can't bring freedom to others if we have not done the hard work of letting Him build His character into us.

This is the same with our lives. If we are ministering from a place of brokenness, we will be pouring from our broken places. We may be spending hours in His presence, but when it comes time to love on others, people will be tasting a mixture of His truth and our hurt. Instead of finding ourselves energized by ministry, we will find ourselves exhausted and run down trying to pour out from our limited strength, as His power drips out through our unsanctified places.

We were made to carry His presence inside of us without leaking. He made us so that He might abide within us, but that only happens when we are made new and the old wineskin is burned away. As the Psalmist writes, "For I have become like a wineskin in the smoke, yet I have not forgotten your statues" (Psalm 119:83, ESV).

When we allow God to refine us in the fire, then He makes us like a new wineskin that He can use. He wants us to be pure vessels that reflect Him fully filtered. Our lives ought to be a cool refreshing drink to a thirsty world of a good God who makes people new.

I have seen too many people minister from a place of brokenness. Because the Holy Spirit is bigger than them, He can and will use them—just like he used King Saul—but the result is not breakthrough and freedom for them, and the fallout of leaders being sanctified in the spotlight has real consequences. It can create a lot of confusion for people who may have mistakenly put them on a pedestal.

We are drawn to charismatic personality types. We see

making new wineskins

the potential for greatness, and it inspires us to follow. In past generations, many burgeoning leaders were given a platform before they were ready. The stories of fallen church leaders continue to trend in the media, and often become a stumbling block to an outside world. God loves us too much to not do the character shaping we need to carry the mantle. Let's deal with our issues before we find ourselves in the spotlight. The platform without character usually does the most damage.

One of my friends was the daughter of such a man. He had a radical testimony of salvation right out of prison. Jesus met him, changed him, and he turned his life around and dedicated it to kingdom work. God lined him up with some influential men of faith, and he began to speak at churches, and even ended up in leadership. He was gifted (dare we say anointed), but behind closed doors his family continued to be dysfunctional. He operated from a place of anger and abuse—places he had never been healed from in his childhood. After years of waiting, praying, and persevering, his wife and daughter were unable to endure any more and left him. Depressed and hopeless, he ended his life with his own hands shortly after. His daughter told me that although he was incredibly gifted, he hadn't let the Lord heal the broken places in him from his past. The anointing of God, which did flow through him, was a temporary one. He missed out on living out the full potential God had for his life. He was charismatic and gifted, but without the character to steward that gifting, our pride will trip us up every time.

I don't know about you, but I don't want that to be my

life's story. *There goes Angelise, so full of promise and potential, and yet…so broken.* For much of my ministry and life, this has been smack dab where I have been—pouring out from my brokenness and my limited strength. But I'm done from pulling from this broken cistern that can not hold water. It's time to let Him restore the broken places that His Spirit has been leaking from. You see, I don't want the Spirit of God to occasionally work through me, I want Him to take up residence and abide within, and this requires letting God do a renewing and a refining in us.

If we want to minister to others in a way that will bring transformation, healing, and breakthrough, it is going to take His fragrance at work in us—the fragrance of humility that is purchased in the pain of endurance and trial.

My Refiner's Fire

My husband and I were a trainwreck waiting to happen. He is an internal processor and not one for hugs and kisses. On the other hand, I need to verbally process every aspect of life and am all about the feels. If that's not enough to sign us up for counseling, let me tell you; I'm just getting started.

Then there's our backgrounds. I was raised by a first generation Filipina American mom who met Jesus at U.C. Berkley, during the 1960s race riots, and a father who was raised off the land and spent most of his childhood in Hawaii and American Samoa. I was homeschooled (when that wasn't a common lifestyle choice) by a family that looked at life outside the box, lived counter-culturally and appreciated our natural God-given systems.

making new wineskins

My father is an electrical engineer and has had many incidents over the years that could have required medical intervention, but I have seen God miraculously heal neck injuries and respiratory issues in his body many times with just the laying on of hands. My favorite personal story of God's miraculous intervention happened when I was just three years old. One of our family friend's sons was pronounced dead in the womb by seven doctors. Knowing nothing of worldly wisdom or the scientific arguments against a miracle, I prayed for him faithfully every night, and one morning, his mother's womb jumped alive with no explanation, to this day, by the doctors. Jesus just showed up and did it. He took the childlike faith of a mother and her community, and He did the impossible. He likes to build our faith like that. That testimony has become so foundational to how I see health and healing.

Surprise! My husband, Matt, was raised exactly the opposite. His parents were by the book All-Americans. His mom was on the PTA, and his father was a partner at one of the biggest law firms in Washington, D.C. They counted the education system and the medical system as a part of their support network. When my mother-in-law was eighteen years old, she was miraculously spared from a tragic car accident where everyone else in the car perished. She underwent six months of reconstruction and PT in the medical system to be able to walk again. She considered the medical establishment providential supply.

Needless to say, in our human strength, with those personality and family differences, our marriage was a combustible explosion waiting to happen.

Americans are professionals at entertaining ourselves to death, and we were no exception. The first three years of marriage we were both busy with our D.C. jobs. We spent a lot of time distracting ourselves from our differences. We were constantly going out, hanging with other people, and spending money on trips and the newest gadgets. It was easy to ignore the differences glaring us in the face.

Once our kids were in the picture, the difference of our backgrounds came rushing to the forefront of our family, and let's just say, every decision became a fight. From a logical and practical standpoint, we were an ill-fitted pair for a harmonious home. But God doesn't want us to be people who lean on our own strength. He intentionally created us so opposite from one another that combined, we actually make a perfect pair. In our differences, He has captured a picture of the diversity of His Body. God's ways are the opposite of what makes sense to our limited human reason. In His love, He had a plan bigger than either of us could begin to imagine.

When our first daughter was born in 2014, the Lord made it very clear it was time for me to put my growing career to the side and raise this little person full time. It was in pulling back and refocusing, that God began to do His work. At first, we were too sleep deprived to realize it, but once the second kid came around in 2016, we had reached a breaking point. We were six years into marriage and we disagreed about everything. We knew something had to give.

making new wineskins

That spring, my health was the first signal that something was off. I became groggy in the afternoons and irritable at the drop of a hat. I saw a chiropractor who called me out on my snacking habits (one of my coping mechanisms), telling me I needed to get those under control.

Our family underwent a six-month detox on a paleo diet, and things started improving regarding how my body felt. I was taking God at His word in surrendering my strength to His higher way (Luke 10:27, NIV).

Then there were the negative self-talk patterns that had to be re-taught. New choices had to be made in the area surrounding my mind's wellness. Dr. Caroline Leaf was instrumental in helping me understand rewiring of my mind and the practical steps that must be made to re-train the makeup of my thinking.[11] As a man thinks, so He is (Proverbs 23:7, NKJV). I hadn't realized how many negative thought patterns I had been sowing into my marriage for so many years. I had started to view my husband in a different light because I had been, in my head, daily labeling him in that way.

In order to do a full 180, I had to figure out how much I wanted it. Let's be honest; I wanted it mostly for my kids at that point. I put myself, my feelings, and my desires for what I wanted from him on the altar and started cultivating friendships, reading habits, and daily checks in my mind to sow the sound mind patterns I wanted to be harvesting when I turned eighty. Thank you to Lara Casey's book, *Cultivate*, and her Powersheets life planner for helping me cultivate what matters.[12] We don't suddenly become something one day. We cultivate and work towards that until it becomes our daily reality.

I'm glad the Lord began this process when He did because if I hadn't surrendered to His leadership, I wouldn't have been ready for what came in the fall of 2018.

The Ultimate Surrender

Cancer. It's the diagnosis no one wants to hear. Yet, it is exactly the soil that God sovereignly handcrafted to answer our prayers and glue our family back together. You see; God had been preparing and healing the soil of my mind and body so I would be ready for the soul and spiritual growth He wanted to do in me next. He builds one layer on top of another.

Faith is not something that happens overnight. It is cultivated little by little over time. It took me a while to realize that the seeming nuisances of the summer of 2018, were all preparation for the cancer diagnosis of our son. The flood in our basement in May, turned into a huge foundation and basement remodel that lasted the whole summer. And my son, Chase, was diagnosed the day after our intense summer of home projects was finished.

The decisions we make to trust God in the midst of life's circumstances help us grow the muscles we need to handle situations in the future. When I chose selfishness and my personal comfort instead of faith and worship, the growth process was painful. When I chose to trust, His peace passed understanding.

People have asked me how I was able to handle my son's diagnosis without trembling with fear. There was definitely the initial moment

making new wineskins

of trepidation when I was asked if I would trust God or not. Each time I was posed that question, I was reminded of how faithful He had been in the little things. He was doing a re-work on my brain. My son facing cancer didn't faze me the way it might have earlier that summer because He was getting a hold of my heart. Slowly but surely, He was showing me that He truly was the one I could depend on for the little and big, and the issues happening around me were not coincidence. There was warfare, and there was shaping, and He was in all of it.

Being the resourceful and redeeming God that He is, my healer started answering prayers for my marriage through our son's journey through cancer. If there was anything that tied the two of us together, it was the love for our son. The desire for his well being was the one thing that we had in common. God also knew that our differences were the perfect ingredients to help our son thrive through cancer.

As I mentioned earlier, I am naturally minded in my health outlook. In fact, I'm prone to just ignore the whole medical community and go off on my own. Have you ever heard about the cancer treatments in Tijuana, Mexico? Let's just say, I was ready to get off the grid and go that route. I've watched too many friends and family members walk away from modern medicine and thrive in their lives because of it. I had also witnessed too many trust their doctors implicitly and pay the price for not doing their own research.

As I mentioned earlier, my husband trusted doctors. He also knew a lot of people on the cutting edge of cancer research. So, what were we to do? With our son's diagnosis, we came to a breaking point. How were our two worlds to collide? Except, they weren't meant to collide. They were meant to join together and blend in such a way that our two different family backgrounds finally became the new family that he and I had started on the day we said, "I do." Our son's diagnosis was when we painfully, truly began the process of saying goodbye to being "members" of our families of origin and started working as a team for the good of this new family God had created.

God put so many unifying people in our way. The first oncologist we met bridged the gap between our two worldviews. She was respected by the medical community, but totally open to new ways of doing health. When our son was cleared to be monitored three months later, she told us with tears how grateful she was for the partnership we'd had that involved supporting our son with options nutritionally and naturally at home. Only God can take something so hard as our conflicting core values and use it as the very environment to do what only He can do: unite us. While this was just the beginning of a very long five-year cancer battle, God was setting the stage to prepare our hearts and the foundation of our home to depend on nothing but Him for our son's good and our family's healing.

The surrendering of my son's life to a medical system I did not trust or prefer was for me the ultimate act of depending on God. I knew I had the resources and people who could help us fight naturally. In fact, just before my son's diagnosis, one of my good friends had successfully shrunk a tumor in her throat simply through overhauling her diet. How I steward medical decisions is a deeply ingrained part of my core values intertwined with

making new wineskins

how I practice my faith. I have also watched God heal people miraculously many times, but learning to submit to my husband and work as a team with him was the refiner's fire for me. I had to trust God with the son I had chosen to birth naturally to avoid him being "tainted" by modern medicine. God told me, "I'm bigger, Angelise, and I'm going to teach you how much bigger I am than even the broken, bureaucratic, toxic medical system."

His ways *are* so much bigger than ours, and He knows our freedom flows from letting go of whatever version of "safety" and "control" our brain depends on and trusting in Him alone.

∽

This journey of transformation and breakthrough has not been overnight. It has been a step by step surrender of letting Him make new wineskins out of my life. I'm just giving you a snapshot of my family's story so that it might provide the framework for you to find your way in your story. My journey of surrendering my son to this medical saga continued into 2020, 2021 and even 2022. Maybe you could say I am hard headed? Or perhaps you realize, as I have, that God has been in every detail. He is so lovingly and patiently removing every layer and false refuge I have outside of Him, so that all that is left standing is Him, my strong tower, fortress and defender!

There is not the time or space in these pages to share the lessons learned (and re-learned) over the past five years, but I pray the lessons in these pages encourage you wherever you stand in your journey. This is not a one and done process. Each new chapter of life, we get to learn the lesson of surrender. Hopefully, the process becomes less traumatic as we realize He is doing something in the tension. Hopefully, we let Him build upon the last lesson instead of repeating the same lessons over and over. When we start to realize that his process of refinement is actually for our good and that He is lovingly revealing areas that need surrender, then we will start to move in the right direction and see His hands in the details of our story.

I've started to count the discomforts of this life as a badge of honor. Yes; this world is broken. However, I've noticed those on the front lines of the spiritual battle live the most interrupted lives. It's as if the Lord allows them to be pushed out of their comfort zone, and the enemy sees their threat to his plans and targets them more hotly. Have you felt the heat, my friends? Count yourself in good company. I know the battle can be exhausting, and I know sometimes you just want to quit and stop fighting the good fight. But be encouraged, He who began it will complete it.

We are limited, and our human strength needs rest, but the enemy wants you to forget that THIS is our secret weapon: His "strength is made perfect in our weakness" (2 Corinthians 12:9, NKJV). When we worship in the midst of the storm, we unleash our greatest threat to the kingdom of darkness; the power of God Himself displayed in the free and unabandoned praises of His people. There is something about saying you trust God even when you don't see the answer yet.

Worship is about showing adoration. What if we were to worship even if we don't "feel" or "see" His sustaining power?

making new wineskins

What if we worship because we choose to see His hand in the details? Our weakness invites His strength. Worship is where we rest. Worship is where we refuel. Worship is where we find immunity from the onslaughts that life brings.

Press on, soldier. Count that target on your back as the highest honor. If we are doing damage to darkness and taking back this earth for His glory, we should expect a lot of discomfort. At the end of our rope is where He steps in, and the *power of God* is displayed for the world to see. The God of angel armies is leading a charge to win souls through the *word* of our testimony, and we get a front row seat in heart transformation and kingdom-shaking power.

The power of
REPENTANCE

The heart is also deceitful. It excuses, rationalizes, and justifies our actions. It blinds us to entire areas of sin in our lives. It causes us to deal with sin using only halfway measures, or to think that mental assent to the Word of God is the same as obedience. We need to ask God daily to search our hearts for sin that we cannot or will not see.
Jerry Bridges

Do we look like Him? Are we drawing others to Him? Or are we the diseased trees that Matthew talks about in chapter 7 of the Gospel, claiming to know Him, but bearing bad fruit?

You will recognize them by their fruits. Are grapes gathered from thorn bushes, or figs from thistles? So, every healthy tree bears good fruit, but the diseased tree bears bad fruit. A healthy tree cannot bear bad fruit, nor can a diseased tree bear good fruit.
Matthew 7:16-18, ESV

What is bad fruit? People who rationalize and justify their actions instead of allowing the Gospel to be applied in their own lives first. People who acknowledge their sin with their heads, but are unable to change in their actions. Are we people who are able to own up to our own need for God? Do we understand the

live out love

power of humility and repentance?

In the last chapter, "Making New Wineskins," we laid the groundwork of my personal place of surrender: trusting God with my son via my husband's different worldview when it comes to healthcare. I hope it stirred in your heart conviction for the areas in your life that you may put a preference before the Kingdom. My view of healthcare was deeply linked to my understanding of my faith, so to separate my conviction for honoring our bodies in the way we choose to treat them from God's higher principle of unity was beyond difficult.

Do you have an area like that in your life that you equate with Gospel truth? Perhaps it has to do with healthcare choices, cultural bias or even your political ideology? At first, we may bristle, but the bristling is a warning sign. Remember when we talked about identifying wake up calls in chapter 7? We are going to take that deeper in this chapter.

The only thing that brought perspective to this seemingly locked tight place of conviction in me was the higher Biblical principle of honoring my husband (and the animation that would arise in me when my worldview was checked). This is a tell-tale sign if you have a stronghold thought pattern in your life: do you get emotional or argumentative when a belief in you is questioned or pushed back against? If someone is making you frustrated, it may not always be the other person at fault.

We all have these blind spots. Whether we lean to the Left or Right politically, prefer to practice health naturally or conventionally, or perhaps it comes down to our parenting ideology: permissive versus authoritarian, we each have our personal biases; the places where we have put our stake in the ground and don't have room for discussion or negotiation. These are our high towers that are getting in the way of God fully moving in our life.

The repeated places of gridlock in our marriage forced me to look at opinions that I had that were in conflict with another person's convictions and ask God, how is this supposed to work? Why am I responding so emotively? If He and I are both in the Body of Christ, and we feel deeply different about this after both laying it at the Father's feet, then what am I missing? Lord, how am I to honor the convictions you have given me and still honor this man you have called me to do life with?

Every couple of months it seems Facebook is on fire with my friends touting two separate Biblical views on the latest cultural issue of the day and throwing seemingly opposing scripture verses at one another on how the other doesn't understand the Gospel. (FYI, the Bible does not contradict itself, but that is a convo for another day). While the arguments are slung back and forth with both sides claiming moral high ground, the world looks at the Church not as God's agent to the world, but a blight to it. We are so busy pointing fingers, we don't see the bad fruit we are labeling in others manifesting in ourselves. (Remember the principle of being judged as we judge from Matthew?) Our hypocrisy has taken away our ability to be agents of change and dampened the Holy Spirit's ability to move in and through us.

So how do you know when you are the one who needs to

take a closer look at things? Check your emotions. Maybe it's a parent who is always making political references that cause you to want to answer back with a heated response. Perhaps it's your spouse who seems to always be dropping comments on your parenting style that make your blood boil. Or do you have a child or teenager who just continues not to listen to a word you say and calls you out on your failure to model what you teach? These are God's gift of grace to you. These are all checkpoints.

God is wooing you to repentance so that you might represent His image better. These are all opportunities He has handcrafted for you to put your faith into action. Does God's higher principle of honoring one another come first, or does your desire to be right? If you are moved to question someone's character and mental soundness based on their preference on masks, vaccines, elections, governmental aid, etc., then maybe it's time to check your heart.

"How is this a marker in my life?" you might ask. If we can question another's humanity on the basis of one of these issues, then we need to check that the Gospel is not just something we "mentally assent" to, as Jerry Bridges' quote mentioned at the beginning of this chapter, but that we actually know how to walk out and obey. Can you consider another as more important than yourself (Phillipians 2:3)? Or is it actually our flesh that is being revealed through these interactions? What do you feel rising in your heart? Self-protection? Do you feel challenged? Disrespected? Unloved? This conflict might actually be revealing a blind spot in you that needs realignment. What fear or pain

the power of repentance

point is this interchange bringing to the surface? That's the area that needs to be surrendered to His Lordship.

The pain points and disagreements we have with others are first and foremost a canvas for the Lord to do His work in us. If there is work to be done in another, He will do it. We can count on it, but it is not our job. Our job is to speak the truth and walk in peace. Our job is to ask the Holy Spirit for a response that reflects His compassion for their sin in light of their need for Christ. Your humility creates the environment for the Holy Spirit to bring conviction to others' blind spots. That ten second pause to consider our own hearts first and then pray for wisdom for theirs is the difference between life and death being unleashed from our tongue, and us getting in the way of His work. If we want the Holy Spirit's conviction to fall where it needs to, we must stay out of the way by not responding in the flesh.

So how do we get from that place of putting our fleshly desires to death to the testimony of others seeing Christ in us? It's the road of repentance, the narrow path of laying down our rights and admitting maybe we don't fully understand the Father's convictions about the issues of our day and age. It's about letting our meekness speak louder than our rights.

God, in His mercy, gives us opportunities to die to our flesh daily that we might bear His fruit. There is a reason why Matthew 7 talking about bearing good fruit (referenced at the beginning of this chapter) is preceded by the Golden Rule: whatever you wish that others would do to you, do also to them (Matthew 7:12). The fruit in our life comes from walking in His principles ourselves and being able to honestly admit when we fall short.

The ingredient that changes the atmosphere in the spirit is our humility. Dying to our flesh, knowing we have a God who loves us and fights for our justice, is where the power of God cocoons itself in the baby-faith of our hearts. The more we cultivate and feed our trust in Him over what we see or hear, the more He is able to step into our circumstances and take the reins in our lives. I don't know how to explain it other than God is for real, and when we train our hearts to put Him first and trust Him most, He really adds all these other things (Matthew 6:33). But someone has to go first.

Who Will Go First?

Who could we find that we have 100% control over? Our kids? Our spouses? If you have been around this globe a couple times, there is one thing that has always been true: There is nobody we can control quite like ourselves.

That is a call to repentance and change, my friends. It starts with us. It always, always, always has to be us. No one else can do it. We have to go first.

It doesn't start with fixing the wrong thinking in that child, that neighbor, that friend. It starts first with us looking at the brokenness in our own hearts and letting God refine and cleanse so we can love people into the kingdom. Something about repentance changes the climate of our atmospheres.

What does that refining process look like? I've heard it said that God will confront things to transform them. In the areas

the power of repentance

where we have spiritual strongholds and ungodly mindsets operating in our lives, we will feel pressure points. The impurities start rising to the surface in the heat of His refining fire. We have one of two choices: roll with the master, or fight the pain and hold on to the cracking, leaking places in our lives.

I mentioned before about my struggle with the medical community and my love of natural remedies, but I didn't realize what an idol of trust this had become to me until I had to come face to face with the medical establishment.

My son's cancer diagnosis and journey taught me so many lessons, but one of the biggest was my inability to trust Him in environments where I could discern idolatry in others. God is so much bigger than medicine and the control and worship of security that our society puts in doctors. So much of our society has replaced its trust and dependence on God, and placed it instead on the so-called "smart people." Instead of trusting a God we can't see, we choose to trust a human who we can. Quick wake up call: they put on their pants just like you and me, guys. They are finite and fallible, just like we are. The doctors on more than one occasion had told us that they were "perplexed" by my son's case. He was a palliative case for years and they couldn't figure out why he was doing so well without following any protocol. I can tell you why, it was because God was at work and he wrote a story in my son's life that didn't follow any medical rhyme or reason. He is the Author and Perfecter of Chase's story.

A misplaced trust in doctors was not my blind spot. Who am I responsible for changing? That's right; myself. My blind spot was conveniently the opposite of my spouse's. I put too much trust in myself and my ability to contact "my people" and do my research with natural remedies. I limited God's ability to work outside of my preferred methods. God was teaching me to trust Him in circumstances and with people who couldn't understand my point of view. God was making it clear that He wanted me to trust Him in the midst of a system in which I could see all the holes and bad practices, walking with faith in the midst.

To clarify, He wasn't asking me to trust in broken humanity. He was asking me to trust *His ability* to walk my family through the brokenness. He was asking me to recognize a higher principle: honor for my husband, who was seeking the best route He understood. And in that proper alignment and trust, I ultimately am trusting in a far higher power that held my son's life in His hands: Jesus.

So what does it look like to go first in repentance? Well, let's go back in time to my son's 3rd MRI imaging after being diagnosed. It was 2018, and I was still new on this surrender journey with the Lord, and the hospital was the last place I wanted to be. When you have already decided to view people in a certain way, they really can't do anything right. I know what it's like to be on the receiving end, but this time, I was on the giving end. For those who have done images and scans with a pediatric patient, you know the frustration with making a precious little one fast first thing in the morning. There we were, two hours into waiting, with a hungry two and a half year old who hadn't eaten since 7pm the night before. I was told that we

the power of repentance

would have to wait another two hours before they could begin the procedure. Two more hours! He could have had water or eaten that morning, if we'd known there was going to be a delay. (Most hospitals allow fluids within 3 hours of sedation). But a two hour wait meant no fluids, and he had already been fasting both food and fluids for over 5 hours since getting up.

I fumed. My flesh got the best of me, and I threatened to call the former head of the hospital, who my husband knew. I immediately called our oncologist and asked her to reschedule the appointment. My husband pointed out the pride of it all. This nuisance was just pointing out one of the old wineskin cracks in my life: control and my lack of trust in God's provision for me and my son. As I apologized to the nurse, I heard the Father tell me: "Finally; now we are getting somewhere."

Had my husband not been bold enough to address that sin issue in me, I would have stayed in a place of bondage. Because He was willing to call it out and potentially take the brunt of my defensiveness, there was an opportunity for me to step into freedom. This is probably the hardest part of repentance. Often, the correction comes from others, and usually, our immediate response is to find something wrong with them instead of us. This is where the Gospel comes into play. Do we believe what Matthew 7 teaches that we are called to look at our own heart first? Will we stay defensive and stay stuck? True; my husband's heart and motivations are not always pure. Do I spend my energy questioning his validity when calling me to check? Or am I more in love with the Lord, wanting to look like Him, therefore willing to accept and wrestle with feedback from others to see if anything resonates?

The Risk of Being Known

It is difficult to be vulnerable and repent; isn't it? Especially when people identifying our blind spots don't always do it from a place of love. It always feels like such a social faux pas to acknowledge our blind spots. Even when I apologized to the nurse, she seemed surprised that somebody would own up to their sin. Our sin nature tells us that if we expose ourselves, we will destroy our standing.

Society praises women who appear perfect on the outside. We never dare show we have imperfections. We can do it all! Social media is littered with children perfectly dressed, no signs of dirt or lunch. In my early 20s, I believed the hype and wondered if some people just had perfect DNA, and I wasn't one of them. Are some people born into perfect families and some not? I've met people who believe that. Somehow they get the parents who knew what they were doing when they made kids, and they are benefiting from this perfect upbringing. I now realize this is one of the biggest tragedies of all. If we play that card, or the opposite and pretend to be a victim of circumstances, we shut down the Holy Spirit's ability to flow in our life. These are both pride in its two extreme forms: narcissism and false humility. It is repentance and the ability to confess our sins that are key to being human and having healthy relationships.

When people live unaware of their flaws, conviction and

the power of repentance

vulnerability are hard to come by. They become masters of shifting the blame and operating in defensiveness if anything is remotely called out in them. When the reality of their humanity hits them, it is often hard to live with the realization of their imperfections. I think it is because they thought their perfection was what made them loveable. It goes back to chapter 2, and our identity. What are we rooted in? If it's ourselves, how can we be loved if we have issues?

I'm not sure if this is universal or just the area I currently live in, but I have been wrestling with this cultural expectation of perfection. I live in northern Virginia, one of the most financially well off and intellectually populated areas. Women are praised when they have it all together. It seems that each family is expected to have no issues. Maybe we don't come out and say that, but it is almost an unspoken standard we hold one another to. I was told once that vulnerability comes across as weakness. Maybe that's why too many of us are afraid to let people see the real us. I was told in confidence once that vulnerability means "people think they can walk all over you." That got me thinking. *Is vulnerability a flaw? Is it better to have everything together?*

Don't get me wrong; we should aim for excellence. I applaud those mamas wanting to share something they are good at with the world. We should seek to have healthy rhythms in our world. We should work toward making healthy meals and teaching our kids the importance of respecting their bodies and making wise choices.

What I'm asking is, does vulnerability make us look weak?

live out love

Does it make society say, "This woman does not have it together." Or is being honest about our need for God and for compassion actually a sign of *strength?*

We brushed very quickly over the concept of our strength being found in acknowledging our need for Him in chapter 7. Let's dig in with a deeper application to this principle. What does it actually look like to admit we don't have it all together, repent of our brokenness and watch God turn it around for our good? How does repenting of our attitude actually set us free? Let me share a simple example of what it looks like to admit our need and find His power.

There have been seasons of my life when repentance was not my go to. I would get so bogged down in my weakness. Instead of crying out to the God who hears and admitting my need for Him to change me, I tried to move forward in my own strength. Every step forward felt like three steps back. Before I came to realize the importance of my identity and the freedom of admitting my lack, these days often put me in a tailspin.

I remember when I was having another one of those days early on in my motherhood journey. I and my two kiddos under three had been sick with a nasty virus for two weeks (This was pre-covid), and I was finally getting my crying minions out of the house for an activity, desperate for something to distract and engage them. We got to a local farm, got out of the car, and everyone melted down. My daughter wanted to hold her ball. She wanted it to fit in the bottom of the stroller. There was a rock in her shoe. Her life was apparently very hard. As

the power of repentance

another mom pulled her two happy kids out of the car, my son's nose started to run for the 100th time that week, as he wailed about the heat. There I was in the baking hot sun, wishing I was somewhere far away.

In my early days of mothering, on days like this, I often had an absolutely rotten attitude. Newsflash: that is usually a huge influencer on everyone who is wailing anyway. "If mama ain't happy, nobody is happy," is a two-edged sword. But when in a place of frustration, usually the last thing we want to do is be real with someone about it. Am I right? We just want them to feel sorry for us and commiserate with our tough situation or frustrating circumstances. At that moment, isn't that what we need most? Relationship. Perspective. Someone to pull us out of ourselves. Someone to lovingly tell us that our attitude needs a fix. How to get there?

It wasn't until I sent out an "SOS" for prayer to my Bible study that things started changing in the spiritual realm. Something about making yourself truly known brings clarity to your issue, and having others pray beside you brings reinforcements to the battle. All of a sudden, I saw the depravity of my heart and my self-centered focus on my problems and lack of love for those around me. All of a sudden, my problems didn't seem as big as the God that I serve. All of a sudden, His love started pouring through my brokenness. My kids could breathe easy again because finally, Jesus, and not I, was on the throne of our home. It took crying out for help to other humans for that ball to start rolling. It took realness and vulnerability. It took community in order for me to change and for me to be an agent of change for others.

Pastor's wife, Christine Hoover, recently talked about these essential ingredients of community in her blog, *Grace Covers Me*. She wrote:

> Revealing ourselves feels risky because it involves embracing weakness and imperfection. Image-keeping feels far less risky because we believe it protects our sensitive areas from the judgment of others. For some reason, we believe impressing other women will lead to connection and community, so we expend effort on building an image rather than revealing ourselves. But until we lay down our defenses, until we stop trying to shield our insecurities and shame from the eyes of others, we will not experience the friendship that goes beyond the surface level, the kind we so long for. Do you want to know a secret? People can see through our defenses anyway. We're not hiding as much as we think. Vulnerability is the way we lay down our arms. Vulnerability takes a weakness and makes it a strength, a bonding agent, because acknowledging our need for God and others attracts fellow vulnerable sojourners like a magnet. Perfection-striving may impress from a distance, but it is vulnerability that wins friends.[13]

When it comes to community, friendships, and being known, it's so important we let our guards down and let people know us for who we really are: weaknesses and all. The downfall of hiding our imperfections is we stay stuck in our sin, and when it is addressed it takes a demolition team to tear down and rebuild. This is the reason why we have doctor check ups and inspectors look at our home. We want to address issues before they become widespread.

The same is true for our souls. You can only avoid the "truth" for so long. If you downplay significant misalignments and keep popping the "pain meds," so to speak, eventually you will find that you have a significant issue. You could have looked for the root cause up front; instead, you pour yourself into therapy, medication and counselors on the back end. If you don't do the maintenance work when things are fine, you will end up with a wall barely standing because the termites of avoidance have destroyed the good things inside.

He wants us to step into our purpose. He wants to see us healed, but if we avoid the character training moments on the front end of our journey, we may have a much tougher go of things. We are called to be quick to repent and see our need for Christ. We are to be people who run to the cross and desire to be in alignment with His fruit of the spirit.

A Repentant Lifestyle Requires Confident Trust

I'm ready for pushback that being vulnerable means you open yourself up to hurt. There are no promises that being real with people will be perfect. In fact, it can get quite messy finding the right people you can be real with. I encourage you to give yourself grace, trust your gut, and look for people with fruit in their lives to speak into you. It's probably also wise to clarify, we aren't called to be 100% vulnerable with all people. We do need an inner circle that we know is for us. We talked about that in chapter 2. Sharing vulnerably with all is less a sign of strength and leans more towards a lack of self-control.

When it comes to being real about your inadequacies to a friend or spiritual mature mentor, that is the essential for community. We need people who love us enough to call out our blind spots. The end goal of not being hurt at all is in itself a faulty goal. A beautiful quote on building trust, from Samuel Johnson, reminds us "It is better to suffer wrong than to do it, and happier to be sometimes cheated than not to trust." We can't shy away from community because we have been hurt. Otherwise, we will never step into true freedom that is found on the other side of humility.

The prayer is that when people realize we don't have it all together, they will choose to grow with us and let their guard down too. It takes a measure of boldness and strength to let people know we are each broken, but it is only when we are real with people that we will experience relationships with others and with Him the way we were designed to.

We must also remember, we aren't just putting our most sensitive places out there for people to attack. We are resting in our identity in Him and His love for us, not their judgment of us. This is why chapter 2, on knowing whose we are is so critical and foundational to understand before we step into this place of humility with others. When we know who we are, we are secure. When we are secure in His love, then we can walk in humility with others - recognizing both our need to be made more like Him, and our eternal security in His unconditional love. When we feel tired, and insecurity rears its head, our job is to run back to our secret place with Him and ask Him to remind us of how He sees us, so we can re-emerge in a relationship with others secure and able to love them in their weakness.

None of this is possible without a Biblical community to remind us when we forget. I don't know what I would have done without my spiritual mom, Ms. Rosa. In moments when the enemy has used those close to me to wound me and try to tear down my identity, I called her, and she would remind me to run to my "safe place" so I could fight and love and prophecy from a place of peace. And that is where the victory flows from; not from my might, but by His spirit. Without His supernatural armor over our hearts, we are sitting ducks for the enemy to destroy. Our humility in hard places must come from a place of rooted trust in our Daddy's love.

Let the Church Live Loudly

My prayer has been one for revival for my local community. "Come Lord Jesus, and set the captives free." Too many marriages are struggling in our culture without a healthy Body to point them back to their first love. Too many kids are walking away from the faith of their parents because they didn't see it lived behind closed doors. Too many unbelievers are looking at the Church as trapped and hypocritical. This should not be. This should not be Christ's Bride.

Christ's Bride is broken and yet washed clean; unfaithful, yet wrapped in His loving kindness and grace. As for the woman at the well, it's His kindness that brings repentance. His truth changed her and set her on a mission. It was fruit that poured out of the heart; transformation that marked her. This fruit could only have come from the work of the Spirit. This could only be made manifest in our lives as our trust in God's faithfulness and love for us increases.

Are we people who actually trust God to move on our behalf?

We may preach it, but our actions show if we believe it. We may tell the world that our God is mighty to save, but when we try to play God by bulldozing over others' convictions to make them hear our perspective, our actions deny it. We may say our God has all power in His hands, but when we try to create a miracle by controlling the environment by which He might work, we are testifying of the opposite

Where are His people who are ready to boldly say, "I'm with Jesus of Nazareth! Me, in all of my mess; I've been changed by the Blood of the Lamb. I was lost, but now I'm found. I was blind, but now I see." My God has miracle working power, and He isn't finished yet! I trust Him in the right now, even when I can't see what's next because faithful is just who He is!

There's something about His power displayed in our weakness. It's when we figure out we bring nothing to the table that He can finally step in and use us as instruments.

∽

I don't know about you, but I'm done with normal "Christianity"—religious rituals void of the power of God. I want to walk in the mantle of His spirit, that He might abide in me and make a residence there. The Holy Spirit is a free gift to all who call on the name of the Lord, but if we don't allow our vessels to be made new, His spirit will leak through the cracks of our unhealed broken places, and our prayers will lack the authority of the power of Heaven. I'm tired of it– of prayers empty of power because I have refused or ignored His prompts to lay myself on the altar and let Him do the pruning He needs to do. Our prayers have power when they come from a vessel surrendered, cleaned out and refined by the Father. It all boils back to repentance, surrender and obedience. "Surely the arm of the Lord is not too short to save, not His ear too dull to hear. But your iniquities have separated you from your God; your sins have hidden His face from you so that He will not hear" (Isaiah 59:1-2, NIV).

Oh; but when we get the surrender right, when we repent and cry out for mercy, His Word says that "times of refreshing come from the Lord" (Acts 3:19, NIV).

> 'For He will come like a pent-up flood that the breath of the Lord drives along. The Redeemer will come to Zion, to those in Jacob who repent of their sins,'
> declares the Lord.
> Isaiah 59:19b-20, NIV

Then, His new wine can be poured into our new wineskins. We no longer leak out but instead overflow with the power of God. Then our prayers are pointed and effective for the pulling down of strongholds. We become catalysts for change in our communities. We see healing flow through our interactions. Our authenticity and humility creates space for God to move.

10

Let my life be
THE PROOF

If I speak with human eloquence and angelic ecstasy but don't love, I'm nothing but the creaking of a rusty gate. If I speak God's Word with power, revealing all his mysteries and making everything plain as day, and if I have faith that says to a mountain, "Jump," and it jumps, but I don't love, I'm nothing. If I give everything I own to the poor and even go to the stake to be burned as a martyr, but I don't love, I've gotten nowhere. So, no matter what I say, what I believe, and what I do, I'm bankrupt without love.
1 Corinthians 13: 1-7, The Message

We can talk all we want, but our walk will be what marks us at the end of the day. Did we live what we preached? Did we love when people spat in our face? I love the band For King and Country's powerful anthem *"Proof of Your Love"* that challenges us to recognize that our actions often carry more weight than our words. If I sing, but with no love, then my breath is wasted. Even if my rhetoric is poised and convincing, without love, my words are a bitter pill.

Oh how this song has convicted me to live with integrity! His truth is planted deep in my soul, but for much of my life, I was a Christian who looked good outside of closed doors, and

live out love

failed to live out the words I spoke behind them. When my duplicity was seen by an outsider, I was mortified.

I convinced crowds and moved Bible study groups with my understanding of the Word, but behind closed doors, my husband had a bitter taste in His mouth because I preached at him the importance of him loving and forgiving me but failed to see that same log in my eye.

One of the hardest lessons of my life was not my son's cancer diagnosis, but in my marriage. You see, my husband and I prioritized our faith differently when we were first married, and my husband was not impressed with my Christian resume: the Bible studies I had led, the women I had helped grow in their faith, or even my daily prayer and time in the Word. Unimpressed.

I struggled with the sovereignty of God. Did I marry the wrong person? Did I mess this one up? How could we grow together as one in our faith if we didn't even view one another's walks as complementary?

God helped me realize this was a gift. I couldn't fake my walk or take the easy way in this marriage. When you are in a marriage that does not understand one another spiritually, it's a whole other level of testing. This test is a gift. The hotter the fire, the more valuable the vessel that makes it through. Ordinary clay can withstand about 1,100°F, but a porcelain piece goes through fire at 2,600°F. Instead of bemoaning the turned up temperatures, I can rejoice knowing He has plans for my life. He uses those hot temperatures to bring out the exquisite piece underneath. I love how Rebekah Lyons puts it: "The measure of trial you've endured directly relates to the measure of hope you offer the world. So press on!"[14]

I had gotten to a point in my life where I thought I had become discredited to do ministry. My marriage didn't look right, and we just weren't on the same page. My dreams of being used for God were dead. But it turns out they were dead to my false idols of ministry and alive to His better plans!

I know God in a way far deeper because my husband challenged me to live every word that I spoke. My husband became a catalyst for change in my life. I understand now that this mountain in my life was the Lord's way of revealing just how deep the imperfections in me went. Matthew West's "*Broken Things*" has become one of my favorite songs, as it reminds me He can use even my story. History is full of imperfect rebels and prodigals that God used. It's the misfit heroes who walk in humility through which God delights and magnifies Himself.

Instead of viewing my scars as a mark of my uselessness, I realized that, refined in the fire, they made me the very tool God could use for supernatural work. "Not by might nor by power, but by my Spirit" and His Spirit alone (Zechariah 4:6, NIV).

As I put to death my dreams of what my marriage could and should do, God was raising a story of a woman who had to find all of her dependence on the God who put the heavens and earth together; a woman not dependent on her own strengths, but on her weaknesses. This made room for God's victory to be magnified in her life.

live out love

Refuting Without a Word

Why did the Christian faith spread so far and wide from a motley crew of uneducated fishermen and tax collectors? Was it the eloquence of the early apostles' words? Was it their good looks and exciting lives? Or was it because even as they were being chased by dogs and torched to death, they continued to declare the glory of the risen Savior? Nothing was stopping the power of the message of the gospel; not even gruesome and painful deaths.

We see in 1 Peter 2, the charge that the early Church was left, in the midst of persecution of the most extreme kind.

> Live such good lives among the pagans that, though they accuse you of doing wrong, they may see your good deeds and glorify God on the day he visits us. Submit yourselves for the Lord's sake to every human authority: whether to the emperor, as the supreme authority, or to governors, who are sent by him to punish those who do wrong and to commend those who do right. **For it is God's will that by doing good you should silence the ignorant talk of foolish people.** Live as free people, but do not use your freedom as a cover-up for evil; live as God's slaves. Show proper respect to everyone, love the family of believers, fear God, honor the emperor. Slaves, in reverent fear of God submit yourselves to your masters, not only to those who are good and considerate, <u>but also to those who are harsh. For it is commendable if someone bears up under the pain of **unjust suffering** because they are conscious of God.</u> But how is it to your credit if you receive a beating for doing wrong and endure it? But if you suffer for doing good and you endure it, this is commendable before God. To this you were called, because Christ suffered for you, leaving you an example, that you should follow in his steps. "He committed no sin, and no deceit was found in his mouth." <u>When they hurled their insults at him, he did not retaliate; when he suffered, he made no threats.</u>
> **Instead, he entrusted himself to him who judges justly.**
> 1 Peter 2:12-23, NIV, emphasis added

Let my life be the proof

What makes a bigger impact than a moving speech or fame? It's a life that is lived 100% committed to one's beliefs. It makes the world take a breath and realize that there is something bigger than the meaningless chase for purpose. When we are mistreated and still choose to honor, when we are given the shorter end of a deal, and yet we sacrifice, that speaks of Jesus' presence.

Peter charges the followers of Jesus, scattered among the pagan world, to live in such a way that, even though the world might accuse them of breaking laws and doing wrong, some might actually come to believe in the risen God because of the actions and lifestyles of the Christians.

In fact, Peter goes so far as to tell them to submit themselves to harsh masters. I can think of some circumstances in my life that felt exactly like that. I felt trapped under authorities that did not understand me and accused me of things I was not doing. For a long time, I pushed against the injustice of it all. When I was disciplined or called out for things I didn't do, or when I was labeled a heretic or hypocrite when I knew I was choosing to love in the face of hate, my spirit would rise with an excuse to prove my rights instead of trusting the Lord to fight for me. Peter reminds the exiles of the example of Jesus and that we should follow in His steps: "'He committed no sin, and no deceit was found in his mouth.' When they hurled their insults at him, he did not retaliate; when he suffered, he made no threats. Instead, he entrusted himself to him who judges justly" (1 Peter 2: 22-23, NIV).

Here is the sinless and perfect Messiah, sent specifically to make a way for the very people crucifying Him, and in His silence against their unjust accusations, He placed Himself in the hands of the most just judge of the universe who holds eternity in His hands. If Jesus could stand there without any blemish as He was accused and attacked, how can we not follow in His steps?

This has gripped me at the most inopportune times. When insults are hurled on me by someone I love, and I'm innocent of their accusations, everything inside of me wants to rise up and defend myself. But on those rare occasions when I allow the words of scripture to penetrate my heart and actions, I have watched God do impossible things. I have watched my accuser drop accusations and instead apologize. I have watched the very thing I longed for become mine without a fight. I have also obeyed in hard moments and seen nothing, trusting God to do His work in His time.

This practice of trusting our lives and justice to a good God is not something that comes overnight. It must involve discipline; cultivated and practiced. It takes time and obedience to become someone whose life testifies to a faithful God. It is not something that can be faked.

Oh; the painful and tiresome and tedious work of creating habits.

Muscle Memory

For much of my childhood I participated in hula and jazz dance classes. I loved the thrill of being on the stage and getting to perform, but I was never a big fan of practicing at home. In fact, I didn't practice much for performances. My thirteen year old self arrogantly wondered why I needed to practice when it was all stored away in my brilliant mind? (If you didn't catch the sarcasm, I hope you know it's dripping thickly.) You see; no one had fully explained to me yet the importance of muscle memory. My teenage self thought many times: "I know the steps. I've seen my teacher do it over and over. Why do I need to keep doing this? Let's move on to the good stuff."

Isn't that how we can look at character-shaping moments in life? We think, "Let's just skip the hard stuff and get to our big moment of glory." It wouldn't be till I was thirty years old that I would realize the same logic flowed into how I did my Christian walk. I read all the books, I went to all the conferences, I knew all the people, I should be good to go; right? So why did I keep running into this wall of my insufficiency?

Yes; I know there is still sin inside. But, you see; I was living in bondage a Christian has the authority to step out of. I was still living in unforgiveness, depression, and anger, but Jesus came to set me free, and the only way I was going to take that mental scriptural knowledge out of my head and put it into practice was repetition.

I didn't know that. It was just supposed to happen. I pray and trust, and God will do the lifting; right? Sadly, no, and too many Christians stay stuck in this place of prophesying breakthrough but never doing the work to steward it. Working our faith out with fear and trembling is something we really should be talking more about. Thoughts create habits in our mind, and those habits in our mind flow into practice in our day to day life.

Breakthrough doesn't just happen because of a pat prayer; though prayer is powerful, and I've seen friends' lives transformed because of it. It doesn't just happen because we will ourselves to be stronger. Change happens when we mentally create daily new habits, have some sort of official or unofficial system to keep track, and then we repeat, repeat, repeat. Then, when we get on stage for that big performance—when the insults are flying, and our flesh feels flush with anger—we don't have to think; our muscles have already created a memory of daily repetition. We can just live in the moment, take it all in, and let Him work through the rhythms of discipline. We trust Him to fight for us. Practice helps us live the life daily that reflects Him and creates space for others to meet Him; even in the face of injustice.

Creating Habits In the Midst of Suffering

It's all well and good to talk about practice, but what about pushing through when you would rather quit? What about those moments when the pain is more than you can take, and you just want to change course and do something else? Believe me, sister! I have been there so many times. How many of us miss out on the good fruit of strong character because we have cut corners in life and taken the easy way out? In Romans 5, Paul writes:

> Not only so, but we also glory in our sufferings, because we know that suffering produces perseverance; perseverance, character; and character, hope. And hope does not put us to shame, because God's love has been poured out into our hearts through the Holy Spirit, who has been given to us.
> Romans 5:3-5, NIV

Let my life be the proof

Did you hear that? We glory in our suffering? Why? Because suffering produces perseverance. What is perseverance besides finishing what we start? It's the pushing through the sweat and pain to finish that workout routine called "the hard knocks of life." Perseverance produces character—the strength to do the right thing when everyone around us is doing the convenient thing. Character gives us the gem called Hope, an unwavering trust in what will be.

We work out because our hope is in knowing the abs are coming. We finish our 9-5 job because our hope is in knowing payday is just around the corner. Hope is not some intangible thing. It is *real*. We just don't have it in our hands at this exact moment.

That is why hope does not put us to shame. The Holy Spirit is our ever present friend, reminding us with little prompts that He is here, and He is with us as we press on to the prize Jesus has called us to: Himself. Oh, what an amazing God He is!

∞

When we die, what will we be remembered for? They may recount the things we accomplished and the awards we won, but what will people walk away with at the end of the day? Maya Angelou has been credited for the quote that "People rarely remember what we say to them, but they always remember how we made them feel." That is a testament to love at work in the soul. Loving people changes people, and love is wrapped in knowing them.

James calls us out in the place we are so prone to wander: "Do not merely listen to the word, and so deceive yourselves. Do what it says" (James 1:22, NIV.)

God has created us to be containers overflowing with His presence; that we might serve a weary world the sweetness of His new wine in us.

He wants to restore and heal us so we might overflow with His Spirit! He longs to pour into us that we might live free as stewards who can not contain His living water! He wants to flow bountifully and freely through us to all those around us, but that happens when we live love loudly. Our witness speaks louder than our words.

11

Our secret WEAPON

> Lift up your heads, you gates; be lifted up, you ancient doors, that the
> King of glory may come in. Who is this King of glory? The Lord strong
> and mighty, the Lord mighty in battle.
> Psalm 24:7-8, NIV

Do we understand who our Daddy is? We serve a risen Savior who conquered death. Not only that, but by His death, we gain a new identity. According to Romans 8, we are now children of the Most High God, and He's a good Daddy-the best! So we know we can approach His throne with confidence; knowing that He hears us and He strengthens those who seek His face. If our imperfect parents do their best to love kids and hear their cries, how much more so will a good and perfect Father? Matthew 7 declares:

> Ask and it will be given to you; seek and you will find; knock and the door will
> be opened to you. For everyone who asks receives; the one who seeks finds;
> and to the one who knocks, the door will be opened. Which of you, if your son
> asks for bread, will give him a stone? Or if he asks for a fish, will he give him
> a snake? If you, then, though you are evil, know how to give good gifts to your
> children, how much more will your Father in heaven give good gifts to those

live out love

> who ask him! So in everything, do to others what you would have them do to you, for this sums up the Law and the Prophets.
> Matthew 7: 7-12, NIV

Jesus was and is the fulfillment of the prophecies of old. He has come, and He has set up His church on earth that "the gates of hell" would not prevail against her (Matthew 16:17-19).

You are no longer a slave, but a daughter or a son! You can ask your Dad with boldness because you know He loves you, and if it's not for your good, He will say "No." But His plans are *for you and for your good!* (Jeremiah 29:11, NLT)

Once we know how to ask of our Daddy with boldness, we can actually do what we are called to do.

Fully Armed

We are not left hopeless and unarmed, as we guard our tongues and wait for God to act. We have a secret weapon that is supernaturally powerful, and it is called *prayer*.

Yeah, yeah; I'm sure you have heard it before. Are you rushing to read the next thing?

We need to stop and realize the power we have literally left at home. We have a good Father who is *for us,* and prayer taps into supernatural resources beyond our understanding or power. Something about prayer activates the Holy Spirit on our behalf.

I'm a fighter by nature. In my culture and family background, you make things happen. If something is wrong, you call it out. If someone wrongs you, you call them to account. Then God started teaching me from Exodus

our secret weapon

14: "The Lord will fight for you; you need only to be still" (Exodus 14:14, NIV).

To be still goes against everything in my go-getter, multitasker, overachiever personality. I have to let someone else get it for me? I have to let someone else fight for me? Fighting for myself had gotten me nothing but frustration, so I finally relinquished control because my way had been leaving me empty handed. Time to try something new.

When someone sins against me now, and I have no control over the situation, I'm learning to lean into His strength. Me trying to call out and convict my husband leads to nothing but more fights and more sin on my part. I am learning to keep my mouth shut; Jesus' example shows that sometimes in enduring, God refines in us a character worth more than much gold. I am learning to stop, look up to God, and let Him know that I trust Him. When there is injustice, I don't always need to make it right. My God fights for me.

Amazingly, He has full-on convicted my husband so many times in the midst of my silence and prayers for defense. He has come to my aid and fought for me.

One of the biggest issues my husband and I have had to walk through is a spirit of unforgiveness towards one another. Sometimes the presence was so tangibly heavy I felt like I couldn't breathe. I remember one time, as we left an oncologist appointment, our medical differences started rising to the surface. We found ourselves at our usual place of bickering and misunderstanding. We have been here so many times.

I felt a heavy presence of a battle of spiritual proportions.

live out love

This was not just him and me misunderstanding one another. What should have been a productive and celebratory doctor's appointment had become a point of marital contention. And it wasn't just "our sin;" there was a devious planner in our midst stirring the pot, and we were picking up on his suggestions.

So instead of continuing to argue, instead of crying, instead of feeling trapped, I began to pray quietly to myself. "In the name of Jesus, I command every evil spirit to leave our vehicle: Accusation, you have no right here. Bitterness, leave, in the name of Jesus. Unforgiveness, you were overcome at the cross. My husband has been washed in the blood of the Lamb, and you have no power here."

The atmosphere of our car began to change. Dissension in the air began to dissipate, and my husband, no joke, turned to me and asked me to forgive him for his unforgiveness and bitterness.

How often do we fail to utilize the weapons at our disposal? Our strength is not found in our wisdom, but His. I recommend every believer get a copy of Priscilla Shirer's war room guide, *Fervent*.[15] Too many of us lack understanding of the significance of the battles we are fighting. The battles are not against flesh and blood, but against spiritual entities in the heavenly realms. So gear up, and start *praying*.

God is Fighting For You

God used my son's cancer story to show me just how big He was, but that wasn't the end of the story. Nine months later, the tumor grew back. We were back at square one, and every doctor was saying the same thing: chemo.

our secret weapon

We had been through this journey. We followed their instructions. The tumor had shrunk 85%, and they had deemed it clear to be monitored. Then, it came back. My little two year old—fighting cancer for the second time.

Believe me; I didn't want to do protocol for protocol's sake. I wanted to look back and know that we had sought the Lord for every decision. In my quiet time with the Lord, I had a very strong sense that this time it was going to be different. *"Behold, I'm doing a new thing,"* is what He was impressing on my spirit.

Yet every single doctor was saying chemo. They were all saying to take the same steps we had taken last year. We even sought new opinions. They were all on the same page.

Was this the Lord confirming? Still I felt Him saying something different to me in our quiet moments together; something that conflicted with what everyone around me was saying. Lord, am I not hearing you right?

Every time I turned on the radio, listened to a podcast or flipped onto my social media, He continued to repeat the same thing to me. The same verse from my quiet time with Him was popping out everywhere I looked:

Forget the former things; do not dwell on the past. See, I am doing a new thing! I am making a way in the wilderness and streams in the wasteland. I will make rivers flow on barren heights, and springs within the valleys. I will turn the desert into pools of water, and the parched ground into springs... that people may see and know, may consider and understand, **that the hand of the Lord has done this,** that the Holy One of Israel has created it.
Isaiah 43:19, 41:18-20, NIV, emphasis added

There was such a strong sense He was in this. We were not

live out love

to dwell on the things He had done before or get caught up in the miracles He had done in the last season. He was doing a new thing, and my eyes were to be laser focused on anticipating His sufficiency in this moment.

Was I to convince them? My husband was pushing for chemo too. Lord, how are you going to move here?

Then one of my church ladies I call for prayer and wisdom said the wisest thing, "If He said He's going to do it, He will do it."

What a lightbulb moment! He's got this. Who am I in comparison to the God who made the heavens and earth? If He can create something out of nothing, can't He fulfill what He is promising to me?

That's the God I serve. I don't have to prove Him or make His will happen here on earth. I just need to listen, follow and obey.

So, I relinquished control. This was not my battle to fight.

Sometimes being a catalyst means waiting on God to do the work in His time, instead of trying to fix it in our time.

When we met with a second surgeon and oncologist, I repeated my concerns about chemo and the fact they were recommending the same treatment we had just walked through nine months ago. I asked again, per the Spirit's promptings, why surgery was not on the table.

Then, I left it there. Me: the type-A fixer, stopped trying to fix it. I don't know what happened other than the Holy Spirit zipped my mouth shut. He had a plan, and not even I was going to get in the way of it. This is what a new identity in Christ looks like. When He says move, I move. When He says stop, I stop. "I

our secret weapon

have been crucified with Christ and I no longer live, but Christ lives in me" (Galatians 2:20, NIV).

I'll never forget the look in the eye the surgeon gave me when he finally understood what I was asking. It went from a routine meeting of him giving official recommendations while looking down at his paper, to him actually hearing. The Spirit of God opened his ears and his heart. He looked up, looked me in the eye and three times said, "I hear what you are saying."

That night I slept with such peace. I knew the Lord was fighting for my son. We had already had two surgeons, one ENT, and two oncologists all give us the same recommendation. Yet God was the one who made these doctors, and He knew what was best for my little guy, and nothing they said would stop this. He was going to do what He said He was going to do.

The very next morning, my husband got a call from the surgeon. They had all changed their minds! It was even the official recommendation from the National Oncology board. All three of these established doctors were now saying surgery was the best route to take. I heard Proverbs 21 echoing loudly in my soul.

> The king's heart is like a stream of water directed by the Lord; he guides it wherever he pleases. People may be right in their own eyes, but the Lord examines their heart.
>
> Proverbs 21: 1-2, NLT

The tumor hadn't even been removed yet, but this moment felt like Christ's victory moment of the story. God was already establishing His glory in the situation, and I was but an onlooker watching Him work. He had plans and purposes for my boy, and nothing was going to thwart that.

One of my friends shared about an intercessory call she was on where my son, Chase, was brought up, and it was prophesied, without them even knowing the details of what had transpired with the doctors decision, that this thing would come out in its entirety with no need for chemo.

I slept like a baby that night. My God was fighting for me.

The surgery was the very next day, and instead of taking the two to three hours they had anticipated, the tumor was removed from his neck in one hour. Not just some of it—they got the entire thing out without impacting the throat, carotid artery, or any other vital structures they had originally been concerned about.

Should I be surprised? He did it! He did exactly what He said He was going to do. *"That people may see and know, may consider and understand, **that the hand of the Lord has done this**"* (Isaiah 41:20, NIV, emphasis added).

This is one of my big Ebenezer moments of life, a stone of remembrance of where God has moved. God was reminding me who is in control of my family's life. Not one detail is out of His control. He is the Almighty One, and He holds life in His hands. Our anthem is one of victory. We must declare God's perspective over our circumstances. To paraphrase Big Daddy Weave in the "*Lion and the Lamb*": Our God is the Lion of Judah. He is roaring over us. He is fighting our battles for us!

Live Out Love

God can move in places we can not. Our trust and surrender makes room for His presence to change circumstances. It is our ability to love like Him when we are being ridiculed and mistreated that breaks down strongholds. When we fight from a place of rooted identity, with our breastplate secure, our kindness can melt the hardest heart. Our patience and listening ear can be a catalyst for His healing presence. Our life is the proof that gives the secret weapons of prayer and trust, a supersonic charge that the enemy can not stand against.

> But even if you should suffer for what is right, you are blessed. "Do not fear their threats; do not be frightened." But in your hearts revere Christ as Lord. Always be prepared to give an answer to everyone who asks you to give the reason for the hope that you have. But do this with gentleness and respect, keeping a clear conscience, so that those who speak maliciously against your good behavior in Christ may be ashamed of their slander. For it is better, if it is God's will, to suffer for doing good than for doing evil.
> 1 Peter 3: 14-17, NIV

The process of preparing to release this book has been a testing over and over of the words I wrote on these pages. I have failed too many times to count. I have tried to fix people and situations in my own strength. I've talked out of turn and tried to force change and revelations in minds and hearts that weren't ready to hear yet. Some of the delay of this book coming out was because I had to go back and clean up messes from my own words and actions. I have had to learn again and again to lean into His strength instead of trying to fight on my own.

I've seen victories surface more regularly, as I have taken a

live out love

moment to breathe, pray, and listen for his rhema word. Our love can break down walls that our preaching never could. Many believe that spiritual strongholds must be torn down with prophetic utterances and well-timed scripture verses. I was one of those people for a long time. I have since learned that love and long suffering have a kryptonite hold on the demonic forces that seek to pull us down. They must bow to the fruits that reveal His spirit at work in us. When we begin to walk like Jesus, they see the mark of our Father on us, and they realize that His kingdom is coming to earth. It changes everything in both the physical and the spiritual realm.

My marriage is still a work in progress, but I trust and believe with each chapter in our story, we are seeing more opportunities to lean into God's faithfulness and what He has already written within the fabric of our lives. We are secure in Him, and when we stay in Him, we have absolutely nothing to fear.

Because we are made in the image of God, every single one of our cells can not help but respond to the eternal reality that He has written. We could no easier reprogram a magnet to no longer have positive and negative ions. We are what we are, and the truth of eternity is what it is because He said it is, and He is the designer. When we begin to walk in alignment with this reality, and when we are faithful to love in the face of attack, it breaks down walls of hostility. The hardest heart longs to be loved and can not fight against its design to be seen and known. So when we love in the face of slander and ridicule and judgment, we win! Love breaks down barriers.

our secret weapon

Our ability to walk in this place of surrender is rooted in our understanding of who our God is. When we know He has all power and authority in His hands and that we are loved by Him, then we can fight from a place of rest and trust. We can face the obstacles and mountains of life from a place of peace. Why? Because we know our God is for us.

I pray you would look at whatever situation is facing you today and know God is intimately involved in every detail. He has not forsaken you, and He is not surprised at where you find yourself. He is standing right there, waiting to move on your behalf. He is waiting for you to make space for Him.

Acknowledgements

The words on these pages would not be possible without an army of people. To my supportive husband, whose friendship is the reason this book even exists, thank you for your faithful refinement in my life. Thanks to you, I am slowly learning the art of listening and giving grace. Thank you for believing in me, being proud of me, and always encouraging my work. Thank you for showing me how to keep my thoughts and words understandable to an earth-bound world. You are the gift I didn't know I needed.

To my children, Adriana, Chase, and Shiloh, you gave Mommy the incentive she needed to push through the hard, dark places. Thank you for being exactly who God made you to be. I'm so grateful He chose me to be your mother here on earth. Your sweet souls are a delight to my heart, and I know the Father rejoices over each of you.

Adriana and Shiloh, even when you are naughty, mommy loves you…always! May you never forget that, and may you come to know the Father's love for you is even greater than you can begin to imagine. I pray you come to know Him deeply and find your contentment and purpose in Him alone.

And to my sweet Chase, now whole and healed with the Lord, I am so honored that God chose your father and I to steward your powerful and precious story. I miss you, but my heart rejoices that you are now free from all pain and with the One that your soul loves.

I am who I am today because of the love of people like my father. This book would not be here if not for his listening ear. I'm also deeply grateful to my mother who has never failed to stop praying for me and taught me the importance of boldly standing before the throne of grace. My faith DNA comes from you. To my baby sister and late brother, who have shaped me, challenged me, and sharpened me like iron on iron: I love you both. I could not have asked for two better sidekicks.

There are so many individuals who have come in and out of my life who have helped me learn lessons along the way; so many who have listened and pointed me to His truth. I can not name you all, but I would be remiss without thanking specifically: Soryda Ring, Joanna Neal, Camillia Dechent, Pattie Williams, Katy Eurich, Michelle Keen, Maria Donnelly, Debbie Nagel, Rosa Sherrod, Pastor JC Sherrod Jr. and Dr. Charles Rasberry for your instrumental work, helping me learn to walk in my new identity.

Ms. Rosa, you are the epitome of a catalyst for healing. You personify what I hope to encourage others to live out on these pages. Your husband is so right; you do open heart soul surgery without us even knowing that's what you're doing.

To my "sister from another mister," Joanna Neal: I am so deeply grateful for your friendship. Thank you for being you and pulling no punches. You are exactly what I needed in my life during my darkest season.

Michele Keen, you are the fire to my wind. I love doing life with you and battling in prayer together. Camillia Dechent, my sister, He has certainly brought our lives together for such a time as this. I'm excited about what He is doing in our midst!

To my book club ladies over the years: you have created a space for me to work through my thoughts and be real and vulnerable about both my struggles and my triumphs. Thank you. You are Church, and you give me a taste of what heaven will be like.

To my sisters at Unveiled and our fearless leader, Connie Padmore. You were right there during that season when God turned over a new leaf. You created a space for me to be vulnerable, and you prayed with me and sharpened me in prophetic and spiritual truth. You are my spiritual family and women I look up to, admire, and love to run fiercely beside.

To my Be The Vessel prayer warriors: Kristin, you have created space for us to war in the secret place. I can't wait to see where God takes you. Debs, you champion others and remind us to hold on daily with child-like trust. You are a gem! Nicole, you are a watchman at your post! Your faithful obedience to stay awake is a hidden treasure. You have inspired and encouraged me on countless occasions. Seulji, your prophetic vision is profound and poetic. Thank you for stewarding your gift so well. Charissa, I wouldn't have met these women without your kindness to make the connection and speak such life at critical moments. You are one of the most compassionate women I have ever been honored to meet. He is at work through you, and we haven't seen anything yet in your story!

To my collab writer group (Meg, Brooke, Ande and Hope), book launch team, and Publishing House, I prayed for each and every one of you. He answers our prayers in His perfect time. We are stronger together! To my fellow UHP author, Kendra Carroll, you are the most amazing cheerleader any girl could have. So grateful for your prophetic words over me and believing in this message even when I wanted to give up. Love being in this launching phase running side by side with you.

To Grace Covenant Sterling, our local church that I have prayed for over the past fifteen years; it's so good to finally be home! Being with people who understand the spirit of God working among us is water to this dry soul. He answers the desires of our hearts in his perfect time.

Most importantly, to the love of my life, Jesus of Nazareth: You pursued me when I was a wretch. As one of my favorite songs, "*Reckless Love*," declares, He is lighting up shadows, climbing up mountains, kicking down walls and tearing down lies in pursuit of us. This book exists because you have been writing these words in my heart for the past thirty years and I'm just figuring out the lessons in all that you have been weaving throughout my life. Thank you for bringing me the clarity and the freedom I so desperately desired. You are my All in All and I adore you with every fiber of my being!

Referenced Resources

Chapter 1 - Oversalted
"Love." Merriam-Webster.com Dictionary, Merriam-Webster, https://www.merriam-webster.com/dictionary/love. Accessed 19 Apr. 2021.

Chapter 2 - You are Loved
Leaf, Caroline. Switch On Your Brain. Baker Books, 2015.
Connelly, Jess. Dance Stand Run. Zondervan, 2017.

Chapter 3 - The Heart Behind it All
Augustine, of Hippo, Saint, 354-430. The Confessions of Saint Augustine.
Connelly, Jess. Dance Stand Run. Zondervan, 2017.
Ibid.

Chapter 4 - Just One Piece of the Puzzle
Casey, Lara. Cultivate. Thomas Nelson, 2017.

Chapter 5 - Work of the Spirit
Olford, Stephen F and David L. Olford. Anointed Expository Preaching. B&H, 1998.
Strong, J. Strong's Concordance. Thomas Nelson, 2010.

Nativity. DVD. Milano: Eagle pictures, 2006.
Shirer, Priscilla. Discerning the Voice of God Bible Study. Lifeway Press, 2017.
Strong, J. Strong's Concordance. Thomas Nelson, 2010.

Chapter 6 - Get out of the Way
Lewis, C.S.. The Problem of Pain. The Centenary Press, 1940.

Chapter 8 - Making New Wineskins
Leaf, Caroline. Who Switched Off My Brain? Ben Publishing, 2006.
Casey, Lara. Powersheets Planners. Cultivate What Matters, 2013.

Chapter 9 - The Power of Repentance
Bridges, Jerry. The Pursuit of Holiness. NavPress, 2006.
Hoover, Christine. Grace Covers Me. Baker Publishing Group, 2017.

Chapter 10 - Let My Life be the Proof
Lyons, Rebekah. You Are Free. Zondervan, 2017.

About the Author

ANGELISE SCHRADER

Born and raised in Ewa Beach, Hawaii, Angelise Schrader is a wife, mom of 4 (one on the way), writer, worshiper, community & faith builder.

After spending 7 years in Washington, D.C., equipping young professionals in their careers and speaking for groups from all over the world, Angelise stepped back to focus on cultivating the wholistic life (mind/body/soul/spirit). She began her blog, Wholistic Ho'Ola (to live whole) in 2018 and *Live Out Love* (her first book) was birthed out of that journey.

Her passion is community building, stirring the Church towards authentic faith, and helping women find freedom as they tap into their God given identities. Her prayer is that every man and woman she crosses paths with would be activated and unleashed into their sphere of influence to be agents of hope and healing.